Barbra Streisand

The Biography

Timeless Talesmith

Table of Content

Introduction

Embark on an odyssey through the extraordinary life of the incomparable Barbra Streisand, an American luminary whose brilliance has left an indelible mark across the vast tapestry of show business. Imagine a narrative so compelling that it transcends the boundaries of time and resonates with audiences spanning generations—a journey that encapsulates the very essence of unparalleled success, multifaceted talent, and an enduring legacy that refuses to be confined by convention.

Born in the dynamic borough of Brooklyn, New York, in the throbbing heart of 1942, Streisand's story unfolds against a backdrop of resilience, tenacity, and unbridled ambition. She emerges not just as a name on the marquee but as a legend, an artist whose impact reverberates through the corridors of entertainment, leaving an indomitable legacy that continues to captivate and inspire.

Picture a childhood marked by dreams as vast as the New York skyline—a young girl with aspirations that soared beyond the ordinary. Streisand's upbringing in a middle-class family, punctuated by the early loss of her father when she was a mere 15 months old, laid the foundation for a narrative steeped in both triumph and tragedy. Yet, it is precisely this crucible of experiences that shaped the trajectory of a woman destined for greatness.

Her foray into the world of entertainment began as a nightclub singer and off-Broadway luminary in the pulsating heart of New York City. Like a siren's call, her original and powerful vocal talent lured in admirers, creating a fan base that foreshadowed the meteoric rise that awaited her. The debut on Broadway with "I Can Get It For You Wholesale" was merely the overture to a symphony of achievements, garnering not just applause but a Tony Award nomination and a New York Drama Critics Poll award.

The musical realm became Streisand's domain, a canvas where she painted masterpieces with her melodic voice. Albums such as "The Barbra Streisand Album" and "The Second Barbra Streisand Album" etched her name in the annals of music history, winning multiple Grammy Awards, including the coveted "Best Album of the Year." Her musical prowess resonated, earning her not just critical praise but public acclaim that echoed across the length and breadth of the United States.

Yet, Streisand's narrative is not confined to the stage; it seamlessly transitions to the silver screen, where her star ascends to new heights. "Funny Girl" stands as a testament to her breakout moment, a cinematic triumph that catapulted her into the echelons of global stardom. The accolades flowed, the awards adorned her mantle, and Streisand became an international "superstar," a title well-deserved.

The cinematic journey traverses through a myriad of genres—musicals, dramas, comedies—each role a testament to her versatility and artistic range. From Gene Kelly's "Hello, Dolly!" to Vincente Minnelli's "On a Clear Day You Can See Forever," Streisand's cinematic repertoire becomes a rich tapestry, woven with the threads of her unparalleled talent.

Amidst the accolades and adulation, Streisand's story takes unexpected turns, marked by personal milestones and a foray into the realm of directorial prowess. "Yentl," her directorial debut, not only showcased her acting prowess but also affirmed her capability behind the camera. The film's beautiful score, composed by Michel Legrand and lyricists Marilyn Bergman and Alan Bergman, stands as a testament to her multifaceted artistic endeavors.

In the realm of accolades, Streisand's journey is one of peaks and valleys. Her album "The Broadway Album" in 1985 emerged as an unexpected runaway success, winning a Grammy Award and rekindling the world's love affair with American musical theater. Despite the success, the Academy's oversight in not nominating her as Best Director for "Yentl" stands as a glaring omission, a so-called "snub" that reverberated through the industry.

The 1990s marked a resurgence—a period of personal records, #1 albums, and a continuous reinvention of her artistic persona. Streisand's ability to capture the zeitgeist continued with her starring role in "The Prince of Tides" in 1991, a film often considered the pinnacle of her screen career. Despite garnering seven Oscar nominations, the elusive Best Directing nomination eluded her once again.

Yet, Streisand's journey is more than a reel of cinematic successes. It is a tapestry woven with threads of activism, philanthropy, and an unwavering commitment to causes close to her heart. Her strong political beliefs in social justice infuse both her professional career and personal life, making her a vocal advocate for change. The Humanitarian Award from the Human Rights Campaign, Honorary Doctorates, and the title of Commander of the Order of Arts and Letters bestowed by the government of France all bear testimony to her impact beyond the entertainment realm.

Streisand's involvement in environmental causes stands as a testament to her dedication to preserving the planet. She endowed a chair in environmental studies in 1987 and donated her 24-acre estate to the Santa Monica Mountains Conservancy. As the lead founder for the Clinton Climate Change Initiative, she brought together major cities worldwide to drive down greenhouse gas emissions.

In almost 50 years of an illustrious career, Streisand's contribution to show business is nothing short of monumental. Her vocal range, her raucous sense of humor, and her ability to seamlessly transition between comedy and drama have garnered her a multi-generational fan base. With each live concert performance, Streisand has not only entertained but also contributed proceeds to benefit programs she ardently supports.

The chapters of Streisand's life unfold in a crescendo of achievements, both personal and professional. From her directing triumphs to her chart-topping albums, her resilience in the face of adversity to her unwavering commitment to social causes, Barbra Streisand emerges not just as an artist but as an icon—a force to be reckoned with.

Join me in turning the pages of this captivating biography, an epic tale that transcends the ordinary and delves into the extraordinary. The story of Barbra Streisand is more than a chronicle of achievements; it's an exploration of the human spirit, an ode to artistic brilliance, and an invitation to witness the magic of a true legend. This isn't merely a biography; it's an immersive experience—a front-row seat to the symphony of a life well-lived, a journey worth celebrating, and a legacy that resonates across the ages.

Chapter 1

Early Life and Background

Barbra Streisand's journey into the world began on April 24, 1942, amidst the vibrant cityscape of Brooklyn, New York. Born to Diana Ida and Emanuel Streisand, her early life set the stage for the remarkable tale of an icon in the making.

Diana Ida, a former soprano, once harbored dreams of a musical career but later found herself embracing the role of a school secretary. Meanwhile, Emanuel Streisand was a dedicated high school teacher, and fate had its way of intertwining their lives at the same educational institution where they first crossed paths. It was within the walls of academia that the threads of Barbra's family story began to weave.

The Streisand family, rooted in Jewish heritage, carried a rich tapestry of cultural influences. Barbra's paternal grandparents embarked on a journey from Galicia, a region that straddled the border of modern-day Poland and Ukraine within the Austro-Hungarian Empire. On the other side of her family tree, her maternal grandparents traced their roots back to the vast expanse of the Russian Empire, where her grandfather held the esteemed position of a cantor.

As Barbra's narrative unfolds against this backdrop of diverse ancestry, her early years were marked by the echoes of her mother's soprano melodies and the academic ambiance where her father imparted knowledge. It was in this dynamic environment that the seeds of a future star were sown.

Brooklyn, with its bustling energy and cultural diversity, played a pivotal role in shaping Barbra's worldview. The city streets became her playground, and the vibrant neighborhoods provided a kaleidoscope of experiences that would later infuse depth into her artistry. The rhythm of life in Brooklyn mirrored the cadence of her burgeoning passion for music and performance.

Despite the challenges of the era, Barbra's childhood in post-war America was a tapestry of resilience and creativity. The Streisand household, like many others, navigated the complexities of rebuilding amidst a changing world. It was within this crucible of transformation that Barbra discovered the power of storytelling through song.

The echoes of her family's immigrant journey, the resonance of her mother's unfulfilled musical aspirations, and the cadence of her father's teachings converged to create a unique symphony within Barbra's soul. Her roots, firmly planted in the rich soil of cultural diversity, became the wellspring from which her artistic identity would emerge.

In the hazy days of August 1943, just a few heartbeats after Barbra Streisand's inaugural birthday celebration, fate dealt a harsh blow – her father, aged merely 34, succumbed to complications arising from an epileptic seizure. This untimely departure, possibly spurred by a head injury sustained years earlier, plunged the family into the clutches of near poverty, leaving them grappling with the harsh realities of life.

The narrative of Streisand's early years is a poignant tapestry woven with threads of struggle and resilience. Her mother, now the sole anchor, found herself navigating the turbulent seas of financial instability, working tirelessly as a low-paid bookkeeper to keep the familial ship afloat. As the winds of hardship blew relentlessly, Streisand's childhood became a canvas painted with hues of longing and deprivation.

Reflecting on those formative years, Streisand opens a window to her soul, revealing a sense of perpetual estrangement. In her own words, she describes the profound sense of being an "outcast" in a world where everyone else's father returned home at the day's end, a stark contrast to her own reality. The void left by her father's absence echoed loudly, casting a shadow over the familial abode.

As Streisand matured, the specter of her father's absence continued to loom large, shaping her worldview and coloring her interactions. "Mine didn't," she laments, a poignant reminder of the void that lingered in the place where paternal presence should have resided. Her mother, valiantly attempting to navigate the intricate dance of survival, found solace in providing sustenance, but the hunger for a different kind of nourishment persisted – a hunger for love and connection.

"When I wanted love from my mother, she gave me food," Streisand reflects, capturing the bittersweet essence of a childhood marked by material provision but starved of emotional abundance. The culinary offerings, while filling the physical void, left an emotional hunger unattended. Streisand's journey through these early years was akin to navigating a labyrinth of unmet needs, a labyrinth that would ultimately shape the contours of her resilience and fuel her ambitions.

Barbra Streisand's journey into the world of entertainment began against the backdrop of a familial harmony infused with music. Streisand's early life was set to the rhythm of her mother's melodic tones. In retrospect, she fondly recalled her mother's "great voice" that resonated semi-professionally on special occasions.

During a candid 2016 interview with Rosie O'Donnell, Streisand shared a vivid memory from her adolescence. At the age of 13, she and her mother embarked on a musical venture that would unknowingly set the stage for her illustrious career. In the quaint Catskills, a tape recorder captured the harmonious collaboration between mother and daughter, immortalizing their shared love for music. It was in this intimate setting that Streisand, even at a tender age, first asserted herself as an artist, marking what she affectionately refers to as her "first moment of inspiration."

The Catskills session not only showcased the blossoming talent of a young Streisand but also unveiled her innate ability to connect with music on a profound level. The experience ignited a creative spark that would eventually fuel her ascent to stardom. Streisand's journey, like the delicate notes on that tape, began to take shape, laying the foundation for a remarkable career in the spotlight.

Family played a pivotal role in shaping Streisand's early years. Alongside her own pursuits, she shared her formative years with an older brother, Sheldon, creating a familial backdrop that further enriched her artistic journey. The tape-recorded melodies echoed the support and encouragement flowing through her household.

The familial composition expanded with the remarriage of Streisand's mother, ushering in a half-sister named Roslyn Kind. Born from her mother's union with Louis Kind in 1950, Roslyn would later make her own mark as a singer. The dynamics of this blended family not only added layers to Streisand's personal narrative but also intertwined their musical destinies in unexpected ways.

Education

At the tender age of five, Streisand embarked on her educational journey at the Jewish Orthodox Yeshiva of Brooklyn. Even then, her brilliance and inquisitive nature were evident, painting a portrait of a young girl destined for greatness. However, her exuberance sometimes got the better of her; she was the kind of student who couldn't resist blurting out answers before the questions were fully posed.

Transitioning to Public School 89 in Brooklyn marked a new chapter for young Barbra. It was during these formative years that she discovered the enchanting world of television and cinema. With dreams that reached beyond the borough's boundaries, she confided, "I always wanted to be somebody, to be famous... You know, get out of Brooklyn." Little did she know, those aspirations would propel her far beyond the city limits.

In the eyes of her neighborhood, Streisand wasn't just another face in the crowd. Her voice became a beacon of recognition, a talent that set her apart. Recalling those early days, she reminisced, "I was considered the girl on the block with the good voice." The stoop in front of her apartment building transformed into an impromptu stage where she, along with other neighborhood kids, showcased her burgeoning vocal prowess.

Practicing her singing became a ritual, often echoing through the hallways of her apartment building. The acoustics of the confined space lent her voice a distinctive quality, a prelude to the melodic journey that awaited her. Streisand's determination and passion were evident in every note, each one resonating with the dreams of a young girl who dared to aim for the stars.

Barbra Streisand's journey into the limelight didn't start on a grand stage; it began in the unassuming setting of a PTA assembly. Picture this: a young Streisand, not yet a household name, captivating everyone with her singing prowess. The audience was enthralled, but notably absent from the fan club was her own mother, a tough critic who didn't easily succumb to the charm of her daughter's talent.

In those early days, Streisand's vocal gift was recognized beyond the confines of school gatherings. Invitations flooded in for her to perform at weddings and even summer camps, showcasing a talent that was unmistakably exceptional. However, not every door swung wide open at first. A pivotal moment came with a somewhat disheartening audition at MGM records when she was a mere nine years old. Despite the setback, Streisand's resilience and determination remained undaunted.

It was at the age of thirteen that the tide began to turn. Streisand's mother, once a stern critic, became a staunch supporter of her daughter's burgeoning talent. Together, they embarked on a creative venture, crafting a four-song demo tape that included timeless tunes like "Zing! Went the Strings of My Heart" and "You'll Never Know." This marked a significant turning point, setting the stage for Streisand's ascent in the world of entertainment.

Yet, her ambitions extended beyond the realm of singing; becoming an actress became her primary goal. The catalyst for this decision was a transformative experience at the age of fourteen. Streisand attended her first Broadway play, "The Diary of Anne Frank," and the impact was profound. The leading lady of the play, Susan

Strasberg, became a source of inspiration, a figure whose acting prowess Streisand aspired to emulate. Fueling her ambition, Streisand delved into the world of literature. Her spare time was dedicated to the library, where she pored over the biographies of celebrated stage actresses like Eleanora Duse and Sarah Bernhardt. Novels and plays became her companions, and she immersed herself in the acting theories of luminaries such as Konstantin Stanislavski and Michael Chekhov.

Barbra Streisand's journey to stardom began in the bustling halls of Erasmus Hall High School in Brooklyn, a place that would shape the trajectory of her remarkable life. In 1956, she walked through those doors with a hunger for knowledge and a passion for the arts that would eventually set her on a path to becoming a global icon.

As a student at Erasmus, Barbra quickly distinguished herself, earning the title of an honor student in modern history, English, and Spanish. But it wasn't just academic pursuits that filled her days; she also found herself drawn to the world of music. Joining the Freshman Chorus and Choral Club, her voice resonated through the hallways, a prelude to the powerhouse vocals that would later captivate audiences worldwide.

Interestingly, within the chorus, fate orchestrated a duet between Barbra and another budding talent, Neil Diamond. Reflecting on those early days, Diamond humorously recalls, "We were two poor kids in Brooklyn. We hung out in the front of Erasmus High and smoked cigarettes." Little did they know that these humble beginnings would be etched in the annals of musical history.

The backdrop of Erasmus High, situated near an art movie house, infused Barbra with a love for films. Her awareness of the silver screen extended beyond casual enjoyment; it was an integral part of her teenage years. The crush she harbored for Bobby Fischer, the 15-year-old US Chess Champion and fellow student, added a touch of teenage longing and complexity to her early narrative.

Summer of 1957 marked a pivotal moment as Barbra stepped onto the stage for the first time at the Playhouse in Malden Bridge, New York. A walk-on role was just the beginning, followed by notable performances as the kid sister in Picnic and a vamp in Desk Set. The spotlight found her, and she embraced it with the fervor of a natural-born performer.

Transitioning into her second year, Barbra took on a night job at the Cherry Lane Theatre in Greenwich Village, immersing herself in the backstage world of the theater. Her senior year brought with it the anticipation of a small part in Driftwood, a play staged in a midtown attic space. These early experiences laid the foundation for what was to come – a career destined for greatness.

In January 1959, at the tender age of 16, Barbra graduated from Erasmus Hall. Despite her mother's pleas to stay away from show business, she embarked on a journey to conquer the stages of New York City. Renting a small apartment in the heart of the theater district on 48th St., she became a relentless force, accepting any role that brought her closer to her dreams. Every casting office became a stepping stone, and every opportunity to perform was a chance to prove herself in the competitive world of showbiz.

Barbra Streisand's early years were a mosaic of passion, determination, and an unwavering commitment to her craft. Little did the world know that the girl from Brooklyn was on the brink of becoming a musical sensation, leaving an indelible mark on the entertainment industry.

Chapter 2

Emergence of a Star

In the gritty streets of Brooklyn, Barbra Streisand's journey to stardom began not in glitz and glamour, but in the everyday struggle for survival. A tenacious spirit fueled by dreams, she embarked on a path that would redefine the landscape of entertainment.

At a mere 16 years old, Streisand found herself fending for herself, grappling with the challenges of independence. Juggling various menial jobs to make ends meet, she faced a transient existence, lacking a permanent address. Her resourcefulness was evident as she slept wherever she could unfurl the army cot she carried, seeking refuge in the homes of friends or any other place she could rest her head.

In moments of desperation, the pull of home led her back to her mother's flat in Brooklyn. There, amidst the familiar surroundings, Streisand could savor the comfort of a home-cooked meal. However, this respite was short-lived, as her mother, taken aback by the unconventional lifestyle her daughter had adopted, implored her to abandon her pursuit of show business. Biographer Karen Swenson vividly captures this tumultuous period, noting that Streisand's mother found her daughter's "gypsy-like lifestyle" alarming.

Contrary to her mother's pleas, these challenges fueled Streisand's determination. Far from being deterred, she perceived her mother's concerns as a catalyst to prove herself on the grand stage. In Streisand's own words, "My desires were strengthened by wanting to prove to my mother that I could be a star." This resolve became the driving force behind her relentless pursuit of a dream that seemed elusive to many.

Streisand's ascent in the entertainment world was marked by breakthroughs that showcased her undeniable talent. Her tenacity paid off, leading to milestones that shaped her burgeoning career. The spotlight beckoned, and Streisand stepped into it with a resilience forged in the crucible of life's challenges.

Behind the scenes, the enigma of Streisand's personal life unfolded. Relationships, both turbulent and tender, wove a complex tapestry. The highs and lows mirrored the crescendos and decrescendos of her melodious voice, creating a narrative that resonated with audiences worldwide.

Barbra Streisand's journey to stardom began with an unexpected opportunity at the Lunt-Fontanne Theater in 1960. As fate would have it, she landed a job as an usher during the run of "The Sound of Music." Little did she know, this would be the stage where her vocal talents would first echo through the theater.

Amidst the bustling excitement of the play, Streisand caught wind that the casting director was holding auditions for additional singers. This marked a pivotal moment in her career, as she mustered the courage to showcase her vocal prowess in pursuit of a job. It was a bold move for someone who hadn't formally considered herself a singer until that point.

Despite the casting director's initial reservations about her fit for the part, he saw potential in Streisand's talent. His encouragement, even in the face of rejection, became a turning point. He suggested she embrace her gift as a singer, urging her to include it prominently on her résumé for future opportunities. This advice would prove to be invaluable as Streisand navigated the competitive landscape of show business.

Barbra Streisand's journey to stardom was marked by a serendipitous moment that changed the course of her life. It all started when she approached her boyfriend, Barry Dennen, with a unique request: to tape her singing. Little did they know that this moment would unravel the extraordinary talent hidden within her.

Dennen, eager to support her aspirations, arranged for a guitarist to accompany her during the recording session. As the playback echoed through the room, Dennen was taken aback by the sheer brilliance of Streisand's voice. In his own words, he described the experience as going "insane" upon hearing her sing. Streisand possessed a voice that was not just captivating; it was breathtaking.

Fueling her newfound enthusiasm, Dennen encouraged Streisand to showcase her talent in a talent contest at the Lion, a vibrant gay nightclub nestled in Manhattan's Greenwich Village. Undeterred by the challenges that lay ahead, she took the stage and performed two songs that left the audience in a "stunned silence." However, the silence was swiftly replaced by "thunderous applause" as she was declared the winner.

The Lion became a pivotal venue for Streisand, providing her with a platform to perform for several weeks. It was during this transformative period that she decided to make a significant change—not just to her career but to her identity. Dissatisfied with her given name, she boldly transitioned from "Barbara" to the more distinctive "Barbra."

In the early stages of her career, Streisand encountered skepticism about her appearance, with some critics suggesting she was "too ugly" to become a star. However, her unwavering determination and confidence defied these superficial judgments. In a world that often demanded conformity, Streisand remained true to herself, refusing to succumb to societal pressures.

One notable aspect of her defiance was her refusal to undergo a nose job, a suggestion she received multiple times. In a world where physical appearance often overshadowed talent, Streisand's refusal to conform became a powerful statement. Her authenticity and commitment to her craft began to set her apart in an industry that was quick to impose standards.

Nightclub Shows

As Streisand took her initial steps into the world of entertainment, the Bon Soir nightclub served as the backdrop for her debut as a professional artist in September 1960. Signed on at $125 a week, she found herself in an upscale environment that was a far cry from her previous experiences. Reflecting on those early days, she humorously recalled, "I'd never been in a nightclub until I sang in one."

The turning point in Streisand's artistic journey came when she caught the attention of Arthur Laurents and became the opening act for comedian Phyllis Diller. This marked the beginning of a trajectory that would see her rise to prominence in the entertainment industry. Streisand's unique talent and captivating stage presence quickly set her apart.

Under the mentorship of her manager, Marty Erlichman, and influenced by her growing exposure to a diverse range of female singers from Dennen's extensive record collection, Streisand began to see the potential for a dual career as both a singer and an actress. The names of legends like Billie Holiday, Mabel Mercer, Ethel Waters, and Édith Piaf filled her musical repertoire.

One song, in particular, played a pivotal role in defining Streisand's mission in the realm of singing—the enchanting "A Sleepin' Bee," composed by Harold Arlen with lyrics by Truman Capote for the 1954 musical "House of Flowers." Streisand described the impact of the song, saying, "The lyrics to that song gave me the three acts of a play that I longed for as an actress." In Harold Arlen, she found a songwriter capable of crafting magnificent melodies that resonated with her artistic vision.

According to biographer Christopher Nickens, Streisand's immersion in the works of other great female singers profoundly influenced her style. She began to embody different emotional characters during her performances, expanding the depth and range of her singing. This transformative phase in her artistic evolution allowed her to connect with audiences on a more profound level.

Streisand's journey was not just about musical prowess; it was also a narrative of self-discovery and the realization of her potential as both a singer and an actress. The synergy between her experiences, the influence of mentors, and the rich tapestry of musical inspiration from female icons shaped the trajectory of her burgeoning career.

Barbra Streisand's journey to stardom was not only marked by her incredible singing talent but also by her evolution as a captivating performer. As she graced the stage at various clubs, including the pivotal stint at the Bon Soir in Greenwich Village, she realized the importance of connecting with her audience on a personal level.

In those early days, Streisand honed her stage presence, seamlessly weaving humor into her performances. What set her apart was the genuine charm of her Brooklyn-bred wit, which resonated powerfully with the audience. The six months spent at the Bon Soir became a transformative period where her singing voice drew comparisons to iconic figures like Judy Garland, Lena Horne, and Fanny Brice.

Streisand's ability to engage the audience between songs became a hallmark of her performances. Leonard Harris, a discerning theater critic, recognized her unique talent, predicting, "She's twenty; by the time she's thirty, she will have rewritten the record books." This prophecy proved accurate as Streisand's conversational prowess evolved, becoming more sophisticated and professional.

Early theatre roles and Broadway debut

Barbra Streisand's journey to stardom was not without its bumps, as evidenced by her early experiences on the New York stage. Embracing her first role in "Another Evening with Harry Stoones," a satirical comedy play, she showcased her acting prowess and delivered two soul-stirring solos. Unfortunately, the show faced a harsh reception, leading to its closure the very next day. However, this setback was merely a prelude to the success that lay ahead.

Enter Martin Erlichman, Streisand's personal manager, and the architect behind her subsequent triumphs. With Erlichman's guidance, she embarked on successful shows in Detroit and St. Louis, setting the stage for a more upscale performance at the prestigious Blue Angel in Manhattan. It was during this period, spanning

1961 to 1962, that Streisand's star truly began to ascend.

In a candid moment with Jimmy Fallon on the Tonight Show, Streisand expressed her gratitude for Erlichman, hailing him as a "fantastic manager" who continued to shape her career even after 50 years. Their partnership was evidently a catalyst for her burgeoning success, providing a solid foundation for her to captivate audiences worldwide.

Beyond the glitz and glamour of the stage, Streisand's personal life and relationships also played a crucial role in shaping her journey. As we delve into the upcoming sections, we'll explore the highs and lows, the triumphs and challenges, that have defined this iconic entertainer's life. From her musical contributions that resonate to this day to her profound impact on the entertainment landscape, Barbra Streisand's story is one of resilience, talent, and an unwavering commitment to her craft.

Barbra Streisand's journey into the spotlight took an unexpected turn when theater director Arthur Laurents spotted her talent at the Blue Angel. It was there that he invited her to audition for a role in the upcoming musical comedy, "I Can Get It for You Wholesale." Little did she know that this opportunity would not only catapult her into the world of Broadway but also lead her to a fateful encounter with then-unknown actor Elliott Gould.

As fate would have it, Streisand landed the role of the secretary to the lead businessman, played by

Gould. The chemistry between them extended beyond the stage, blossoming into a love story that unfolded during rehearsals. Their connection transcended the footlights, and soon, they found themselves sharing a modest apartment. The curtains rose on March 22, 1962, at the Shubert Theater, marking the debut of "I Can Get It for You Wholesale." The reception was nothing short of extraordinary, with rave reviews echoing through the theater.

Streisand's performance had an electrifying effect, described by Nickens as having "stopped the show cold." Even the legendary Groucho Marx, while hosting the Tonight Show, acknowledged the remarkable achievement, noting that 20 was an "extremely young age to be a success on Broadway." The accolades poured in, earning Streisand a Tony Award nomination and the prestigious New York Drama Critic's prize for Best Supporting Actress.

The success of the show didn't stop at the theater; it transcended to the recording studio, where the production was immortalized in the form of an album. Streisand's star was rising, and her multifaceted talents were gaining recognition not just on stage but also in the realm of music.

Early television appearances

Barbra Streisand's foray into the entertainment world took a significant turn with her first television appearance on The Tonight Show, back in April 1961. At the time, the show was hosted by the renowned Jack Paar, although during this particular episode, the charismatic Orson Bean stood in for Paar. It was on this televised stage that Streisand showcased her vocal prowess, delivering a mesmerizing rendition of Harold Arlen's "A Sleepin' Bee."

The impact of her performance was undeniable, and it didn't go unnoticed. The legendary comedian Phyllis Diller, who happened to be a guest on the show that night, couldn't help but shower Streisand with praise. Diller boldly declared her as "one of the great singing talents in the world", a sentiment that would resonate with audiences worldwide as Streisand's star continued to rise.

Following her noteworthy appearance on The Tonight Show, Streisand's journey in the television realm continued to unfold. In 1961, she found herself becoming a semi-regular presence on PM East/PM West, a talk and variety series hosted by the dynamic duo of Mike Wallace and Joyce Davidson. This marked the beginning of Streisand's exploration of the talk show format, a platform that would become instrumental in shaping her public image.

Interestingly, around the same time, Streisand was gearing up for her role in Another Evening With Harry Stoones, a testament to her versatility as both a singer and an actress. The fusion of her acting skills with her vocal prowess set the stage for what would become a multifaceted and enduring career.

Delving into the archives of PM East, fragments of Streisand's segments have been preserved in the form of audio recordings. Still photos capture frozen moments of her dynamic presence on the show. However, the moving images, the very essence of her animated performances, unfortunately, remain elusive. It's a reminder of the ephemeral nature of television history and the irreplaceable charm Streisand brought to the screen.

In the early months of 1962, Barbra Streisand made her mark in the Columbia Records studio, laying down tracks for the cast recording of 'I Can Get It for You Wholesale.' That same spring, she lent her voice to a special 25th-anniversary studio rendition of 'Pins and Needles,' a beloved musical rooted in the 1930s by the International Ladies' Garment Workers' Union. Critics couldn't help but rave about Streisand's stellar performances on both albums, recognizing her burgeoning talent and unmistakable presence.

May of 1962 brought Streisand to The Garry Moore Show, a pivotal moment where she delivered a soulful rendition of "Happy Days Are Here Again" for the very first time. This rendition, transforming the once upbeat anthem of the Democratic Party from the 1930s into a hauntingly poignant melody, swiftly became her signature song during these early stages of her career.

The Tonight Show, hosted by the legendary Johnny Carson, served as a significant platform for Streisand's burgeoning fame. Carson, enamored by her talent, invited her onto his show multiple times throughout '62 and '63. Streisand's performances not only captured the hearts of Carson's audience but also won over the affections of the host himself. He labeled her an "exciting new singer," a testament to her magnetic stage presence and undeniable skill.

Her appearances on the show were not only about the music. Streisand showcased her wit and humor, engaging in banter with renowned figures like Groucho Marx. Her unique style of humor left an indelible mark, further endearing her to audiences and fellow entertainers alike during these early days of her burgeoning career.

These milestones served as the launching pad for Streisand's ascent in the entertainment world. Her magnetic performances, signature renditions, and ability to charm audiences and hosts alike laid the foundation for the illustrious career that was yet to fully unfold. Each stage appearance and recording became a stepping stone, propelling her toward becoming an iconic figure in the world of entertainment.

In December 1962, Barbra Streisand graced the stage of The Ed Sullivan Show, marking the beginning of a series of appearances that would skyrocket her into the limelight. The dynamic energy she brought to her performances quickly caught the attention of audiences nationwide. This was just the start of a phenomenal journey that would define her career.

Not long after, Streisand found herself not just a guest but a cohost on The Mike Douglas Show, leaving an indelible mark on the television landscape. Her charisma and talent also became a staple on Bob Hope specials, showcasing her versatility across various platforms. One notable collaborator during this period was none other than Liberace, who, after witnessing her magnetic stage presence, became an instant fan. This admiration led to an invitation for Streisand to dazzle audiences as his opening act at the iconic Riviera Hotel in Las Vegas.

Liberace's invitation marked Streisand's introduction to the West Coast, solidifying her presence as a force to be reckoned with in the entertainment industry. The performance at the Riviera Hotel was not just a gig; it was a stepping stone that propelled her career to new heights. Audiences were captivated by her powerful voice, commanding stage presence, and undeniable star quality.

As her career soared, Streisand found love amid the glitz and glamour of the showbiz world. In September of the following year, amidst her ongoing shows at Harrah's Hotel in Lake Tahoe, she and actor Elliott Gould took a momentous detour to Carson City, Nevada, to exchange vows. The marriage was more than a personal commitment; it became a stabilizing influence in Streisand's whirlwind life. Despite the demands of fame, she saw her partnership with Gould as a source of grounding and support.

The marriage, like her career, became a fixture in the public eye. Streisand's ability to balance her personal life with her soaring professional success added an intriguing layer to her public persona. Fans were not just witnessing a rising star on the stage; they were witnessing a woman navigating the complexities of love and fame.

The convergence of personal and professional milestones painted a vivid picture of Barbra Streisand's life—a life marked by a meteoric rise in the entertainment world and a commitment to love that stood the test of time. As her journey unfolded, it became clear that Streisand was not just a singer; she was a cultural icon in the making. The tale of her ascent was only beginning, and the world was eager to see what the next act would bring.

First albums

Barbra Streisand's journey into the music industry was marked by a bold move at the age of 21 when she signed a contract with Columbia Records. Unlike many artists of her time, she negotiated a unique clause that granted her full creative control over her work, even though it meant accepting less financial compensation. Looking back on this pivotal moment nearly three decades later, Streisand emphasized the significance of this clause in her career:

"The most important thing about that first contract – actually, the thing we held out for – was a unique clause giving me the right to choose my own material. It was the only thing I really cared about. I still received lots of pressure from the label to include some pop hits on my first album, but I held out for the songs that really meant something to me."

This bold decision to prioritize artistic expression over commercial interests became a recurring theme in Streisand's career, as she took advantage of this creative control multiple times.

Columbia Records initially proposed naming her debut album "Sweet and Saucy Streisand," but Streisand, exercising her control, insisted on a more straightforward title: "The Barbra Streisand Album." Her reasoning was simple and pragmatic, as she explained, "if you saw me on TV, you could just go [to the record shop] and ask for the Barbra Streisand album. It's common sense." This strategic move paid off as the album not only reached the top 10 on the Billboard chart but also secured three Grammy Awards, solidifying her status as the best-selling female vocalist in the country.

In the summer of 1963, Streisand continued her momentum with the release of "The Second Barbra Streisand Album." The album not only reinforced her standing in the music industry but also garnered praise, with some hailing her as the "most exciting new personality since Elvis Presley." This rapid ascent to fame prompted Streisand to cap off the breakthrough year with a series of one-night concerts in various cities, including Indianapolis, San Jose, Chicago, Sacramento, and Los Angeles.

Streisand's ability to navigate the complex music industry landscape while maintaining artistic integrity set the stage for a remarkable career. Her insistence on choosing material that resonated with her, rather than succumbing to industry pressures, endeared her to audiences and established a unique voice in the world of female vocalists.

As she continued to shape her career, Streisand's success was not confined to the recording studio. Her influence expanded into other realms, making her a cultural icon. The journey from negotiating a groundbreaking contract to becoming a Grammy-winning artist showcased Streisand's determination and resilience in an industry that often demanded compromise.

Return to the stage

Barbra Streisand's triumphant return to Broadway in 1964 marked a pivotal moment in her career, captivating audiences with her spellbinding performance as the iconic entertainer Fanny Brice in "Funny Girl" at the illustrious Winter Garden Theatre. It was a theatrical extravaganza that not only showcased Streisand's exceptional acting prowess but also unveiled two songs that would become etched in the annals of musical history – "People" and "Don't Rain on My Parade."

The show's instant success catapulted Streisand to unprecedented heights, earning her the coveted spot on the cover of Time magazine, a testament to her newfound stardom. Although she faced stiff competition in the form of a Tony Award nomination for Best Leading Actress in a Musical, Streisand's brilliance shone through, securing her a place as a nominee alongside the legendary Carol Channing in "Hello, Dolly!" While the award eluded her grasp that year, Streisand's contributions to the stage were not overlooked, as she was later bestowed with the prestigious honorary "Star of the Decade" Tony Award in 1970, a fitting acknowledgment of her lasting impact on Broadway.

Not content to confine her brilliance to the American stage, Streisand took her act across the pond in 1966, where she reprised her role in "Funny Girl" to resounding acclaim at London's West End, gracing the Prince of Wales Theatre with her undeniable presence. This international success further solidified her status as a global sensation, transcending borders with her magnetic performances.

Stepping beyond the footlights and onto the small screen, Streisand made her mark in the television realm from 1965 to 1968, starring in a series of solo specials that captivated audiences nationwide. One such gem, the Emmy Award–winning "My Name is Barbra," showcased not only her musical prowess but also her ability to connect with viewers on a personal level, earning her accolades and further solidifying her status as a multifaceted entertainer.

Beyond the glitz and glamour of the stage, Streisand's life was a tapestry woven with both triumphs and tribulations. Her journey unfolded against the backdrop of a rapidly changing world, and she navigated the complexities of personal relationships with grace and resilience. As the spotlight intensified, so did the challenges, but

Streisand's indomitable spirit and unwavering commitment to her craft propelled her forward.

Chapter 3

The Journey to Fame

Barbra Streisand's journey to fame is a mesmerizing tale woven with the threads of musical brilliance and unyielding determination. With an astounding discography of 50 studio albums, the majority under the banner of Columbia Records, she carved her place in the annals of music history.

In the early 1960s, Streisand's musical prowess took center stage with debut albums like "The Barbra Streisand Album," "The Second Barbra Streisand Album," and "The Third Album." These works, now considered classics, showcased her unique interpretations of theatre and cabaret standards. One standout was her rendition of "Happy Days Are Here Again," a departure from its usual uptempo flair. This iconic piece became even more unforgettable when performed in a duet with the legendary Judy Garland on The Judy Garland Show. Garland, recognizing Streisand's vocal prowess, hailed her as one of the last great belters, solidifying her status among the musical elite. Together, they harmonized on timeless tunes like "There's No Business Like Show Business," with the incomparable Ethel Merman joining in for an unforgettable performance.

The transition from television specials to contemporary musical terrain marked a pivotal moment in Streisand's career. While her earlier albums, starting with "My Name Is Barbra," were often medley-filled treasures, 1969 ushered in a new era. Streisand embraced more contemporary material, navigating uncharted waters with the evolving sounds of the day. Despite the dominance of rock music, Streisand's vocal prowess remained steadfast, leading her to a resounding triumph with the Richard Perry-produced album, "Stoney End," in 1971.

The eponymous title track, penned by the talented Laura Nyro, emerged as a major hit for Streisand, cementing her relevance in the pop and ballad-oriented landscape. This marked not only a musical triumph but also a testament to Streisand's ability to reinvent herself and embrace new musical horizons.

In the vibrant rhythm of the 1970s, Barbra Streisand's musical prowess soared to unprecedented heights, painting the pop charts with a kaleidoscope of unforgettable melodies. Tracks like "The Way We Were," a soul-stirring anthem that claimed the coveted US No. 1 spot, became the soundtrack to an era, echoing in the hearts of millions. Streisand's presence was undeniable as she graced the charts with chart-toppers like "Evergreen (Love Theme from A Star Is Born)," a ballad that etched itself into the romantic fabric of the decade.

But it wasn't just individual success that marked Streisand's journey; it was her ability to collaborate seamlessly. The 1979 hit "No More Tears (Enough Is Enough)" showcased her unparalleled chemistry with Donna Summer. This electrifying duet not only clinched the US No. 1 spot but also stood the test of time, retaining its title as the most commercially successful duet well into the new millennium.

Streisand's artistic versatility extended beyond the realm of solo performances. "You Don't Bring Me Flowers," a poignant collaboration with Neil Diamond, held its own atop the charts, resonating with audiences on a profound emotional level. The song, reaching the summit of US No. 1, became an anthem of heartbreak and resilience.

The silver screen became a canvas for Streisand's musical narratives. Tracks like "The Main Event" danced off the soundtrack recordings of her films, capturing the essence of the stories she brought to life. As the curtains fell on the 1970s, Streisand stood tall, crowned as the most successful female singer in the U.S. Only the colossal figures of Elvis Presley and The Beatles had cast longer shadows over the realm of album sales.

Amidst the changing tides of the music industry, 1980 heralded a milestone for Streisand with the release of her magnum opus, "Guilty," produced by none other than Barry Gibb. This collaboration birthed timeless hits, including "Woman in Love," a chart-topper that reigned over the pop charts in the fall of 1980. "Guilty" and "What Kind of Fool" further solidified the album's legendary status, etching Streisand's name in the annals of musical history.

Barbra Streisand: The Biography

Barbra Streisand's return to her musical-theater roots marked a significant shift in her artistic journey. Despite Columbia Records' reservations about deviating from pop songs, Streisand, empowered by her contractual creative control, asserted, "I've always had the right to sing what I want". The result was the 1985 masterpiece, "The Broadway Album," an unexpected triumph that not only secured the coveted No. 1 Billboard position for three consecutive weeks but also earned a quadruple platinum certification.

In a dazzling display of vocal prowess, Streisand took on tunes by iconic composers such as Rodgers and Hammerstein, George Gershwin, Jerome Kern, and the venerable Stephen Sondheim. Sondheim, in a unique collaboration, reworked some of his songs exclusively for this recording, adding an extra layer of brilliance to an already stellar collection. The resounding success of "The Broadway Album" translated into critical acclaim, with a Grammy nomination for Album of the Year and Streisand clinching her eighth Grammy as Best Female Vocalist.

Following the triumph of "The Broadway Album," Streisand continued to captivate audiences with the release of the live album "One Voice" in 1986. Anticipation was high for another Broadway-focused album in 1988, but this project took an unexpected turn. Working under the direction of Rupert Holmes, Streisand recorded several tracks, including renditions of classics like "On My Own" from "Les Misérables," a medley

39

featuring "How Are Things in Glocca Morra?" and "Heather on the Hill" from "Finian's Rainbow" and "Brigadoon," and "All I Ask of You" from "The Phantom of the Opera." However, dissatisfaction with the project led to its abandonment, leaving only "Warm All Over" and a revamped, radio-friendly version of "All I Ask of You" released on Streisand's 1988 album, "Till I Loved You."

The early 1990s saw Streisand shifting her focus to film directing, leading to a period of relative inactivity in the recording studio. In 1991, a monumental release, the four-disc box set titled "Just for the Record," offered a comprehensive retrospective of Streisand's illustrious career. Featuring over 70 tracks, the compilation spanned live performances, greatest hits, rarities, and previously unreleased gems, providing a multifaceted exploration of Streisand's musical evolution.

In the aftermath of Streisand's impactful concert fundraising events in the early '90s, her involvement took an intriguing turn into the realm of politics. The year following, Streisand's efforts played a pivotal role in propelling President Bill Clinton into the political spotlight and ultimately into the highest office in the nation. This wasn't merely a footnote in her story; it was a chapter that showcased Streisand's ability to extend her influence beyond the stage and into the corridors of power. In a moment of historical significance, Streisand herself took the stage at Clinton's inauguration in 1993, solidifying her presence not only as a musical icon but as a force to be reckoned with in the political arena.

As the political curtain drew back, Streisand's music career, though momentarily paused, was destined for a resurgence. The early '90s marked a period where Streisand's focus on live performances hinted at a shifting mindset. A notable appearance at an APLA benefit in 1992, coupled with the memorable inaugural performance, hinted at the singer's willingness to embrace the live stage once more. The idea of a tour began circulating, suggesting a return to the spotlight that fans had eagerly awaited. Streisand, however, hesitated to commit immediately, citing a well-known adversary—stage fright—and legitimate security concerns.

Amidst this contemplation, Streisand found her way back to the recording studio, gracing her fans with the release of "Back to Broadway" in June 1993. While the album didn't receive unanimous acclaim, it achieved a remarkable feat, debuting at the No. 1 spot on the pop charts. This accomplishment was particularly noteworthy given Streisand's seasoned status in the industry, and notably, it edged out Janet Jackson's "Janet" from the top spot. One of the album's shining moments was a captivating medley featuring "I Have A Love" / "One Hand, One Heart," a poignant duet with Johnny Mathis, a singer Streisand openly hailed as one of her personal favorites.

This artistic collaboration not only showcased Streisand's versatility but also underscored her ability to weave a narrative through music. The medley became a standout piece, resonating with audiences and serving as a testament to the enduring power of Streisand's voice. The return to the recording studio and the subsequent success of "Back to Broadway" marked a triumphant chapter in Streisand's career, affirming her lasting impact on the music industry.

In 1993, music critic Stephen Holden hailed Barbra Streisand's cultural standing, comparing it to the iconic Frank Sinatra. This acclaim set the stage for Streisand's remarkable return to the spotlight after 27 years. The announcement of her first public concert appearances created a buzz that transcended her Las Vegas performances from 1969 to 1972. What started as a two-night New Year's extravaganza at the MGM Grand Las Vegas evolved into a sensational multi-city tour in the summer of 1994.

The anticipation surrounding Streisand's comeback was palpable, with tickets for the tour selling out in an astonishingly brief timeframe—less than an hour. It wasn't just a tour; it was an event that captured the imagination of fans and media alike. Major magazines featured Streisand on their covers, with Time magazine dubbing it "The Music Event of the Century." The tour's impact extended beyond the stage; it became one of the most significant all-media merchandise phenomena in history.

The financial magnitude of the tour matched its cultural significance. Ticket prices ranged from a modest US$50 to a staggering US$1,500, making Streisand the highest-paid concert performer in history at that time. "Barbra Streisand: The Concert" became the top-grossing concert of the year, garnering accolades such as five Emmy Awards and the prestigious Peabody Award. The televised broadcast on HBO etched its mark in history as the highest-rated concert special in HBO's three-decade-long legacy.

As the curtain fell on the tour, Streisand opted for a musical hiatus, redirecting her focus toward acting, directing, and nurturing a blossoming romance with actor James Brolin. The success of her comeback tour not only solidified her status as an entertainment icon but also showcased her ability to captivate audiences across generations.

Streisand's ability to reinvent herself, coupled with her enduring appeal, set the stage for a remarkable chapter in her career. The concert not only marked a triumphant return but also underscored her versatility as a performer. It wasn't just about the music; it was a testament to Streisand's cultural impact and her ability to command the stage with unmatched charisma.

In the wake of the tour's triumph, Streisand's musical hiatus didn't dim the glow of her star. Instead, it fueled anticipation for her next move, leaving fans and critics alike eager to witness the next evolution in her storied career. As the spotlight shifted, Streisand embraced new opportunities, solidifying her legacy not just as a singer but as a multifaceted talent who continued to shape the entertainment landscape.

Streisand's journey, marked by highs and lows, triumphs and challenges, is a testament to the enduring power of her artistry. The concert not only revitalized her career but also redefined what it meant to be a legendary entertainer. The echoes of her performances continued to resonate, reminding the world that, in the realm of entertainment, Barbra Streisand was not just a name; she was a force that transcended time and left an indelible mark on the hearts of those who experienced the magic of her music.

In the late '90s, Barbra Streisand's career experienced a revitalization, marked by notable musical endeavors and a return to the spotlight. The 1996 release of "I Finally Found Someone," a poignant duet with the talented Bryan Adams, not only earned an Oscar nomination but also soared to #8 on the Billboard Hot 100. This musical gem was a crucial milestone, breaking Streisand's nearly decade-long hiatus from significant hits and securing her first top 10 position since 1981. It also marked her inaugural gold single.

The magic continued in 1997 when Streisand, after a brief hiatus, graced the recording studios once again, presenting to the world "Higher Ground." This album, a compilation of loosely inspirational songs, included a powerful duet with none other than the sensational Céline Dion. The result? Another No. 1 debut on the pop charts, reaffirming Streisand's enduring influence on the music scene.

As the late '90s unfolded, Streisand's personal life took center stage with her marriage to James Brolin in 1998. Undeterred by the joyous union, she ventured into the studio in the subsequent year, giving birth to "A Love Like Ours." However, critical reception was a mixed bag. While some praised the album, others lamented the syrupy sentiments and overly lush arrangements. Yet, amid the diverse opinions, one track shone brightly— "If You Ever Leave Me," a country-tinged duet with Vince Gill, emerged as a modest hit, further showcasing Streisand's versatility.

Stepping back into the limelight, Streisand's artistic journey in the late '90s was not just about music. In 1996, she unveiled her directorial prowess in "The Mirror Has Two Faces," a film in which "I Finally Found Someone" played a significant role. This venture added a cinematic layer to her multifaceted career, proving that Streisand's creativity knew no bounds.

The allure of Streisand's career lies not just in her musical achievements but also in her unwavering commitment to social causes. Beyond the studio and the silver screen, she dedicated herself to philanthropy and activism. This dedication is not a recent development; it has been woven into the fabric of her life and career.

Streisand's impact on popular culture extends far beyond the charts. The late '90s were a testament to her ability to evolve and adapt, maintaining relevance in an ever-changing industry. As her biography unfolds, the chapters from this era reflect not only the ups and downs of a celebrated career but also the resilience and innovation that define Barbra Streisand.

Barbra Streisand's triumphant return to the concert stage on New Year's Eve 1999 marked a spectacular comeback. The tickets for her performance sold out within a few hours, a testament to her enduring popularity. As the clock struck midnight ushering in the new millennium, Streisand stood at the pinnacle of female singers in the U.S. An incredible achievement, she had secured at least two No. 1 albums in each decade of her illustrious career.

In 2000, a two-disc live album titled "Timeless: Live in Concert" was unleashed, capturing the magic of her stage presence. The enchantment of Streisand's performance reached beyond borders, with renditions of the Timeless concert captivating audiences in Sydney and Melbourne, Australia. This global musical journey showcased her timeless appeal and unwavering influence.

As the applause echoed, Streisand made a surprising announcement in September 2000. She declared her retirement from public concerts after four upcoming shows, two in Los Angeles and two in New York. The news left fans in awe, and her farewell concert featured a memorable performance of the iconic song "People," broadcasted on the Internet via America Online. It was a poignant moment in music history, marking the end of an era in live performances.

The subsequent chapters of Streisand's musical odyssey continued with albums that reflected the depth and diversity of her artistry. "Christmas Memories" (2001) took a somber turn, offering a collection of holiday songs that resonated with emotion. Streisand's ability to infuse her unique style into every genre was showcased in "The Movie Album" (2003), where she lent her voice to famous film themes, backed by a grand symphony orchestra.

In 2005, Streisand embarked on a creative collaboration with Barry Gibb, releasing "Guilty Pleasures" (titled "Guilty Too" in the UK). This album served as a sequel to their previous successful collaboration, "Guilty." The timeless blend of Streisand's vocals with Gibb's musical genius resonated worldwide, reaffirming her ability to craft music that transcends generations.

Streisand's journey through the early 2000s not only showcased her musical prowess but also highlighted her versatility in navigating different genres with finesse. Each album became a chapter in the evolving narrative of her storied career, captivating audiences with the richness of her voice and the emotional depth she brought to every note.

Barbra Streisand's musical journey continued to resonate powerfully in 2006, marked by a memorable collaboration with the legendary Tony Bennett. Their rendition of "Smile," recorded at Streisand's Malibu home, became a soul-stirring addition to Bennett's 80th birthday album, Duets. The magic of their musical synergy was not confined to the studio, as they captivated audiences with a live performance captured by director Rob Marshall for Tony Bennett: An American Classic.

Airing on NBC on November 21, 2006, this televised spectacle was more than just a concert; it was a testament to the enduring allure of Streisand's voice and stage presence. The live duet with Bennett served as the opening act, setting the tone for an unforgettable evening celebrating the magic of two musical icons.

Streisand, never one to rest on her laurels, made headlines with a bold announcement in the same year – her intention to embark on a tour aimed at both raising funds and awareness for various societal issues. The curtain rose on the 2006 Streisand concert tour on October 4 at the Wachovia Center in Philadelphia, following four days of rigorous rehearsal at the Sovereign Bank Arena in Trenton, New Jersey. The tour continued its sonic journey with a notable stop in Sunrise, Florida, and reached its crescendo at the Staples Center in Los Angeles on November 20, 2006.

A touch of grandeur accompanied each performance, with special guests Il Divo seamlessly woven into the fabric of the show. Streisand, then 64, defied conventional expectations, grossing an astounding $92,457,062. The tour etched its name in the annals of box office history, setting records in 14 of the 16 arenas it graced. Notably, the October 9, 2006, show at Madison Square Garden secured Streisand the third-place record, with the first and second spots held by her groundbreaking shows in September 2000.

However, not all accolades came without controversy. Streisand found herself under the critical lens for what some deemed as exorbitant ticket prices, reaching upwards of $1,000. The financial success of the tour prompted discussions about the intersection of art, entertainment, and accessibility. Despite the critique, Streisand's ability to command such prices only underscored her unparalleled status as an artist with a magnetic pull on audiences, transcending mere entertainment to become a cultural phenomenon.

The tour's impact went beyond financial figures, solidifying Streisand's legacy as a trailblazer in the realm of live performances. The MGM Grand Garden Arena bore witness to her second-place record, with her December 31, 1999, show reigning supreme as the highest-grossing concert of all time. As the curtains fell on the 2006 tour, Streisand had not only created an indelible mark on the charts but had also left an enduring imprint on the hearts of fans around the world.

Barbra Streisand's musical odyssey continued to captivate audiences during her 2006 tour, and the live recordings from this enchanting journey manifested in "Live in Concert 2006." This masterpiece made an impressive entrance onto the prestigious Billboard 200, securing the 7th spot and marking Streisand's 29th Top 10 album – a testament to the enduring allure of her performances.

Venturing beyond the familiar shores of North America, Streisand embarked on a landmark series of concerts in continental Europe in the summer of 2007. The tour kicked off in the picturesque city of Zürich on June 18, creating a ripple of excitement that echoed through subsequent stops like Vienna, Paris, Berlin, and more. The air was charged with anticipation as Streisand graced stages that had never felt the power of her voice before.

The European leg of the tour included a historic visit to London, where Streisand had not performed since before 2007. The city welcomed her with open arms, hosting three unforgettable concerts on July 18, 22, and 25. The cultural significance of these performances was mirrored in the range of ticket prices, spanning from £100.00 to a staggering £1,500.00. Ireland, too, had the privilege of experiencing Streisand's magic, with tickets ranging from €118 to €500.

However, not every note played in this symphony of events was harmonious. The Irish chapter of the tour faced logistical challenges, with serious parking and seating issues tarnishing the otherwise enchanting evening. Hot Press went so far as to dub the event a "fiasco," highlighting the hitches that momentarily eclipsed the brilliance of Streisand's artistry.

What made these concerts truly extraordinary was the accompaniment of a 58-piece orchestra. Each note resonated with precision, creating a sonic tapestry that elevated Streisand's performance to new heights. The orchestral grandeur added a layer of sophistication, transforming each venue into a haven for music enthusiasts.

Beyond the melodic celebration, Streisand's 2006-2007 tour became a cultural bridge, connecting diverse audiences across the European continent. It wasn't merely a series of concerts; it was a shared experience, a musical pilgrimage that united people through the universal language of song.

As Streisand's star continued to shine brightly, her impact on the entertainment landscape reached unparalleled heights. The tour wasn't just a showcase of her vocal prowess; it was a testament to the enduring relevance of her artistry. Streisand's ability to traverse continents and captivate audiences with her timeless classics spoke volumes about the transcendent nature of her music.

Amidst the applause and standing ovations, Streisand's personal and professional journey unfolded. The stage became a canvas, and each concert was a stroke in the portrait of a woman who had conquered the hearts of millions. Behind the scenes, her life and relationships formed the backdrop, adding depth to the narrative of an artist who had faced challenges and triumphs with equal grace.

In the dynamic world of music, Barbra Streisand stands as a powerhouse, not just in her vocal prowess but also in her business acumen. In 2008, Forbes recognized her as the second-highest-earning female musician, a testament to her enduring influence and popularity. With earnings reaching an impressive $60 million between June 2006 and June 2007, Streisand demonstrated that her impact extends far beyond the stage.

Undeterred by time, Streisand's journey continued as she delved into her 63rd album in November 2008. This venture marked not just a continuation of her musical legacy but also a collaboration with the talented Diana Krall, adding a fresh perspective to her rich discography. The year also brought prestigious honors, as Streisand became one of the distinguished recipients of the 2008 Kennedy Center Honors. Her influence resonated even in the hallowed halls of the White House, where she participated in ceremonies on December 7, 2008.

Television audiences were treated to a special showcase of Streisand's live prowess on April 25, 2009, when CBS aired "Streisand: Live in Concert." This captivating special featured highlights from her 2006 North American tour, particularly a memorable stop in Fort Lauderdale, Florida. The reach of her performances expanded further as she graced the historic Village Vanguard in New York City's Greenwich Village on September 26, 2009, for a one-night-only show. This remarkable performance, captured on DVD as "One Night Only: Barbra Streisand and Quartet at The Village Vanguard," stands as a testament to her enduring appeal and ability to command the stage.

September 29, 2009, marked the release of the studio album "Love is the Answer," a collaboration once again with the skilled Diana Krall. Streisand's timeless voice found a new canvas in this album, showcasing the depth and maturity of her artistry.

The British audience got a taste of her charm on October 2, 2009, when she made her television performance debut on "Friday Night with Jonathan Ross" to promote the album.

The impact of "Love is the Answer" was nothing short of historic. Debuting at an impressive No. 1 on the Billboard 200, it not only reaffirmed Streisand's relevance but also marked a milestone in her career. With this achievement, she etched her name in the annals of music history as the only artist to secure No. 1 albums in five different decades. The album's success, boasting her highest weekly sales since 1997, attested to Streisand's unwavering ability to captivate audiences across generations.

In a harmonious blend of compassion and talent, Barbra Streisand etched her mark on the sands of philanthropy. On February 1, 2010, she united with over 80 fellow artists to breathe new life into the 1985 charity anthem, "We Are the World." Conceived by Quincy Jones and Lionel Richie to commemorate the 25th anniversary of its original recording, fate intervened with a seismic event.

The devastating earthquake that shook Haiti on January 12, 2010, altered the course of plans. Streisand, alongside the cadre of artists, pivoted their purpose. The song evolved into "We Are the World 25 for Haiti," debuting on February 12 as a heartfelt anthem, a lifeline of support for the beleaguered island nation.

Such gestures of solidarity not only showcase Streisand's musical prowess but also underscore her unwavering commitment to making a positive impact beyond the stage. Recognition for her humanitarian endeavors came to fruition on February 11, 2011, when she was bestowed the esteemed title of MusiCares Person of the Year. This accolade, a testament to her enduring influence, preceded the 53rd Annual Grammy Awards by two days.

In the same illustrious year, Streisand lent her voice to "Somewhere" from the Broadway classic West Side Story. A poignant duet unfolded as she collaborated with the young prodigy, Jackie Evancho, marking a mesmerizing moment captured on Evancho's album, "Dream with Me." Streisand's ability to seamlessly bridge generations with her musical prowess echoes her timeless impact on the industry.

Beyond the spotlight, Streisand's personal and professional life intertwine in a symphony of highs and lows, triumphs and challenges. The chapters of her journey unfurl, revealing the intricate tapestry of her existence. From the early days, navigating the labyrinth of the entertainment industry, to the pinnacle of success, Streisand's life is a narrative that resonates with aspiration and relatability.

Yet, amidst the glitz and glamour, Streisand's unwavering commitment to social causes remains a beacon of inspiration. The power of her voice extends beyond the notes and lyrics, echoing in the corridors of charitable initiatives. From contributing to the revitalization of a timeless anthem for a cause to being at the forefront of

MusiCares' recognition, Streisand's philanthropic ventures amplify her impact far beyond the stage.

Barbra Streisand's captivating journey through the limelight extends far beyond the stage. In an unforgettable moment on October 11, 2012, she took center stage at Barclays Center in Brooklyn, a triumphant return to her roots for the first-ever public performance in her home borough. The three-hour extravaganza, a jewel in her Barbra Live tour, mesmerized an audience of 18,000.

The star-studded event saw Streisand accompanied by the soulful tones of trumpeter Chris Botti, the enchanting Italian operatic trio Il Volo, and the special inclusion of her son, Jason Gould. It wasn't just a concert; it was a symphony of emotion, with Streisand paying heartfelt musical tributes to the late Donna Summer and Marvin Hamlisch, luminaries who had bid farewell earlier in 2012.

The luminaries in attendance added an extra layer of glamour to the already sparkling night. From the likes of Barbara Walters, Jimmy Fallon, and Sting to Katie Couric, Woody Allen, and Michael Douglas, the crowd reflected a constellation of stars. Even the mayor of New York City, Michael Bloomberg, couldn't resist the allure, joining the ranks of designers Calvin Klein, Donna Karan, Ralph Lauren, and Michael Kors.

As if that wasn't enough, Streisand continued her global resonance with two memorable concerts at Bloomfield Stadium, Tel Aviv, in June 2013. The echoes of her performances reverberated through the hearts of fans worldwide, solidifying her status as a truly international icon.

What sets Streisand apart is not just her vocal prowess but also her unapologetic embrace of technology. A notable advocate for using teleprompters during live performances, she stands proudly among a select group of singers who employ this modern tool. In response to any raised eyebrows, Streisand passionately defends her choice, emphasizing the utility of teleprompters not only for displaying lyrics but also for injecting spontaneous banter into her shows.

Streisand's use of teleprompters is a testament to her dedication to delivering flawless performances, ensuring that every lyric and every word reaches the audience with the intended emotion. It's not about relying on a crutch; it's about enhancing the connection between artist and audience, making each moment memorable.

This dedication to perfection is a recurring theme in Streisand's illustrious career. Her commitment to excellence is not confined to the stage; it permeates every aspect of her life. From her early days, marked by a breakthrough in the entertainment industry, to the pinnacle of success where she continues to command global attention, Streisand's journey is a masterclass in resilience, talent, and reinvention.

The concert at Barclays Center wasn't just a performance; it was a chapter in the ongoing narrative of Streisand's life. A life woven with threads of triumph, tribulation, and an unwavering commitment to her craft. The music didn't just fill the arena; it resonated through the hearts of those in attendance, creating an indelible imprint of an iconic moment in musical history.

Barbra Streisand's musical journey is a tapestry woven with success and innovation, a melody that spans over six decades and resonates with the harmonies of collaboration. In September 2014, she orchestrated a symphony of talent with her album "Partners." A melodic masterpiece, it featured duets with musical legends such as Elvis Presley, Andrea Bocelli, and Stevie Wonder, creating a magnum opus that transcended generations.

The resonance was immediate—Partners soared to the pinnacle of the Billboard 200, an illustrious accomplishment that marked Streisand as the sole artist to claim a number-one album in each of the last six decades. The curtain rose on her unparalleled artistry once again, captivating listeners with an album that sold a staggering 196,000 copies in its inaugural week. This triumph not only etched her name in the annals of music history but also bestowed upon her the title of the artist with the most gold and platinum albums—52 gold and 31 platinum, to be exact—surpassing all her female peers.

But Streisand is not one to rest on her laurels. In May 2016, she teased the world with another enchanting project—Encore: Movie Partners Sing Broadway. This tantalizing offering, set to release in August, promised a Broadway-infused serenade with a star-studded cast. A prelude to this musical journey was the nine-city concert tour, Barbra: The Music, The Mem'ries, The Magic, where Streisand's voice, like a siren's call, echoed in iconic venues from Los Angeles to the heart of Brooklyn, her hometown.

The crescendo continued into June 2018, with Streisand unveiling her next studio album, Walls. Released on November 2, 2018, just days before the U.S. midterm election, the album bore witness to Streisand's foray into the political landscape. The lead single, "Don't Lie to Me," resonated as a poignant critique of America's political climate during the tumultuous presidency of Donald Trump. Streisand, with her lyrical prowess, crafted a musical commentary that mirrored the sentiments of a nation grappling with uncertainty.

The title track, "Walls," became a symbolic anthem, alluding to Trump's persistent calls for a border wall with Mexico. Streisand, in her signature style, transformed her music into a powerful narrative, a lyrical canvas painted with the hues of social commentary. The album, a testament to her artistic evolution, showcased Streisand's ability to seamlessly blend music and message, transcending the boundaries of mere entertainment.

As we traverse Streisand's musical landscape, it becomes evident that her artistry is not confined to notes and melodies; it is a reflection of the ever-changing cadence of society. With each album, she orchestrates a symphony of emotion, a harmonious exploration of the human experience. Streisand's ability to infuse her work with social and political relevance is a testament to the transformative power of music.

In this musical odyssey, Streisand's voice becomes a beacon, guiding us through the intricacies of the human condition. Her melodies are not just notes; they are stories woven into the fabric of our collective consciousness. As we await the next stanza in her musical journey, one thing remains certain—Barbra Streisand, with her timeless artistry, continues to be a maestro, conducting the rhythm of our hearts.

Acting

Barbra Streisand's transition from the Broadway stage to the silver screen marked the beginning of a dazzling film career. Her cinematic debut, a reprisal of the Broadway sensation "Funny Girl" (1968), directed by the seasoned Hollywood maestro William Wyler, not only captured the essence of her stage triumph but also proved to be a resounding success both artistically and commercially. In a historic moment, Streisand clinched the 1968 Academy Award for Best Actress for her stellar performance, sharing the honor with Katharine Hepburn for "The Lion in Winter" in an unprecedented tie, etching her name in the annals of Oscar history.

As the spotlight continued to shine on Streisand, her subsequent ventures into film showcased her versatility and love for musical narratives. "Hello, Dolly!" (1969), a cinematic adaptation of Jerry Herman's musical, saw Streisand collaborating with the legendary Gene Kelly, creating a vibrant spectacle on the big screen. The following year brought another musical exploration with "On a Clear Day You Can See Forever" (1970), based on the compositions of Alan Jay Lerner and Burton Lane, and directed by the illustrious Vincente Minnelli.

Diversifying her filmography, Streisand embraced the comedic realm with "The Owl and the Pussycat" (1970), a delightful cinematic interpretation of the Broadway play. This marked a departure from musicals, revealing her ability to seamlessly navigate various genres and captivate audiences with her multifaceted talent.

Beyond the glitz and glamour of the silver screen, Streisand's personal and professional life intertwined in a fascinating tapestry. Her journey unfolded against the backdrop of not just cinematic accolades but also the nuances of relationships and the challenges that came with stardom. The dichotomy of her public persona and private struggles added depth to the narrative, making her a relatable and compelling figure in the eyes of her admirers.

Streisand's ascent in the film industry mirrored her impact on the broader cultural landscape. Her musical contributions transcended the boundaries of entertainment, resonating with audiences far and wide. As she continued to shape and redefine the industry norms, Streisand's influence became synonymous with pushing artistic boundaries and challenging conventions.

Parallel to her illustrious career, Streisand dedicated herself to philanthropy and activism. Beyond the glitz and glamour, her commitment to social causes showcased a different facet of the icon. Whether advocating for humanitarian efforts or championing charitable causes, Streisand's influence extended beyond the stage and screen, leaving an indelible mark on society.

In the whirlwind era of the 1970s, Barbra Streisand graced the silver screen in a series of unforgettable screwball comedies that left audiences in stitches and clamoring for more. Films like "What's Up, Doc?" (1972) and "The Main Event" (1979), where she shared the spotlight with the charismatic Ryan O'Neal, showcased Streisand's versatility and comedic brilliance. Another gem from this period was "For Pete's Sake" (1974), a delightful collaboration with Michael Sarrazin that further solidified her status as a cinematic force to be reckoned with.

However, it was in the drama genre that Streisand truly left an indelible mark, especially with her role in the poignant "The Way We Were" (1973) alongside the handsome Robert Redford. This performance not only captivated audiences but also earned her a well-deserved Academy Award nomination for Best Actress. As if that weren't impressive enough, she clinched her second Academy Award for Best Original Song, teaming up with lyricist Paul Williams for the iconic "Evergreen" from "A Star Is Born" in 1976, a film in which she also took center stage.

Amidst her stellar acting career, Streisand, in collaboration with legends like Paul Newman, Sidney Poitier, and later, Steve McQueen, pioneered the First Artists Production Company in 1969. This groundbreaking venture empowered actors to shape their destinies, secure coveted properties, and spearhead movie projects. Streisand's inaugural foray with First Artists resulted in the thought-provoking "Up the Sandbox" (1972), showcasing her commitment to pushing creative boundaries.

Unveiling her prowess not only in front of the camera but also behind the scenes, Streisand dominated the Top Ten Money Making Stars Poll from 1969 to 1980. An annual fixture in the motion picture exhibitors poll of Top 10 Box Office attractions, she notched an impressive ten appearances, often standing as the lone woman on this prestigious list. Her ability to draw audiences and command box office success became an enduring hallmark of her illustrious career.

The early '80s marked a shift in Streisand's cinematic journey, with the commercially lackluster "All Night Long" in 1981 prompting a reevaluation of her film trajectory. Despite this ebb, Streisand remains a cinematic luminary, having graced the silver screen in a select few films since. Her discerning choices and unwavering commitment to quality over quantity showcase the depth and integrity of her artistic vision.

Barbra Streisand's journey in the world of cinema is nothing short of extraordinary, marked by resilience, creativity, and a determination to break barriers. Director John Huston, in a 1985 Playboy interview, expressed his admiration, stating, *"I'm impressed with her choosing Yentl; it was extraordinary. But for some reason, Hollywood turned against her... there was a lack of sympathy toward her... Christ, she could have played Cleopatra better than Liz Taylor, with her enormous power and the subtlety of her singing... She is one of the great actresses and she hasn't been well used."*

In 1972, Streisand ventured into film production, establishing Barwood Films. Her first cinematic creation, Yentl (1983), faced rejection from multiple Hollywood studios. Undeterred, Streisand not only took on the directorial role but also starred in the film. It wasn't until Orion Pictures embraced the project, allocating a budget of $14 million, that Yentl came to life. This marked the beginning of Streisand's triple-threat role as producer, director, and star—a feat she would later repeat with The Prince of Tides (1991) and The Mirror Has Two Faces (1996).

Yentl, a film that pushed boundaries and challenged norms, garnered controversy when it received five Academy Award nominations. Surprisingly, none were in the major categories of Best Picture, Actress, or Director. Yet, Streisand's perseverance and creative vision shone through, solidifying her status as a trailblazer in the industry. The Prince of Tides followed suit, earning numerous Oscar nominations, including Best

Picture and Best Screenplay, though not for the director.

The accolades and nominations only tell part of the story. Streisand's impact extended beyond the silver screen, resonating with those she collaborated with. Pat Conroy, the screenwriter of The Prince of Tides and author of the novel from which it was adapted, showered Streisand with praise, declaring her "a goddess who walks upon the earth" upon the film's completion. Such sentiments underscored the profound influence Streisand wielded in the creative process.

Streisand's foray into producing her own films wasn't merely a career move; it was a bold statement that echoed her refusal to be confined by industry norms. Her ability to navigate challenges, secure funding for unconventional projects, and deliver performances that left a lasting impact set her apart.

As a multifaceted artist, Streisand seamlessly balanced the roles of creator and performer. Yentl showcased her prowess not only in front of the camera but also behind it, illustrating her directorial finesse. The controversy surrounding the film's Academy Award snubs only fueled Streisand's determination to challenge the status quo.

The Prince of Tides, another jewel in Streisand's filmography, further highlighted her ability to bring narratives to life with depth and emotion. The recognition garnered by the film, despite its directorial omission, underscored the enduring impact of Streisand's creative contributions.

In the words of John Huston, Streisand's talent transcends the limitations Hollywood may have imposed on her. The director's remark encapsulates the sentiment shared by many who recognize her as a force in the industry—an actress who possesses the rare combination of enormous power and the subtlety of her singing.

Barbra Streisand, an icon in the entertainment industry, is not only celebrated for her captivating performances but also for her remarkable contributions behind the scenes. One aspect often overlooked is her role as a co-scriptwriter for "Yentl" alongside Jack Rosenthal. Despite her significant involvement, she sometimes doesn't receive the credit she deserves, as noted by The New York Times editorial page editor, Andrew Rosenthal. It's a fascinating glimpse into the intricacies of Streisand's multifaceted talents, showcasing her not only as a performer but also as a creative force in shaping cinematic narratives.

In 2004, after an eight-year hiatus from film acting, Streisand made a triumphant return in the comedy "Meet the Fockers," a sequel to "Meet the Parents." Sharing the screen with an ensemble cast that included Dustin Hoffman, Ben Stiller, Blythe Danner, and Robert De Niro, Streisand added her unique flair to the film's comedic dynamics. This marked a pivotal moment in her career, reaffirming her versatility as an entertainer who could seamlessly transition between various genres.

A further testament to Streisand's creative pursuits lies in her involvement with Barwood Films, Gary

Smith, and Sonny Murray. In 2005, they acquired the rights to Simon Mawer's book "Mendel's Dwarf." This venture showcased Streisand's interest in diverse storytelling, exploring narratives beyond the realm of her own performances. It's a compelling aspect of her career that highlights a deep appreciation for storytelling in its many forms. In December 2008, Streisand expressed her contemplation of directing an adaptation of Larry Kramer's play "The Normal Heart," a project she had been dedicated to since the mid-1990s. This commitment to socially relevant and impactful storytelling aligns with Streisand's broader influence in the industry, not only as an entertainer but also as a force for meaningful narratives that resonate with audiences.

The year 2010 saw Streisand reprising her role in "Little Fockers," the third installment of the "Meet the Parents" trilogy. Once again sharing the screen with Dustin Hoffman, she brought her character, Roz Focker, back to life. This film not only added another chapter to a beloved series but also showcased Streisand's enduring appeal in the world of comedy.

Streisand's journey encompasses much more than the spotlight of Hollywood. Her foray into scriptwriting, production, and the exploration of diverse narratives speaks to a multifaceted artist who continually pushes boundaries.

In the ever-evolving tapestry of Barbra Streisand's life, the year 2011 marked a cinematic milestone that added a touch of comedy to her illustrious career. The Hollywood Reporter, on January 28th of that year, echoed the excitement that reverberated through the entertainment world—Paramount Pictures had given the green light to a road trip comedy titled "My Mother's Curse." The twist? Seth Rogen would be stepping into the shoes of Streisand's character's son, injecting humor into their on-screen dynamic.

Guiding this cinematic journey was Anne Fletcher, a director known for her knack for capturing the essence of human connections. The script, a creation of the talented Dan Fogelman, promised to intertwine laughter and heartfelt moments. Behind the scenes, a powerhouse team, including luminaries such as Lorne Michaels, John Goldwyn, and Evan Goldberg, collaborated to bring this comedic vision to life. Streisand, not merely content in her acting role, assumed the role of executive producer, ensuring her creative fingerprint left an indelible mark.

As the cameras rolled in the spring of 2011 and wrapped their final scenes in July, the project took on a new identity—The Guilt Trip. A title that hinted at the intriguing twists and turns audiences could expect in this cinematic journey. The road movie, co-financed by David Ellison's Skydance Productions, promised not just laughter but a poignant exploration of the complex dynamics between a mother and her son.

December 2012 saw the culmination of this cinematic venture, as The Guilt Trip hit the silver screen. Audiences found themselves immersed in a world where Streisand's comedic finesse met Rogen's endearing charm, creating a delightful tapestry of laughter and emotion. The film's release was not just a testament to Streisand's enduring star power but also a testament to her ability to reinvent and diversify her artistic portfolio.

Beyond the glitz of Hollywood premieres and red carpet events, this project exemplified Streisand's willingness to explore uncharted territories. A road trip comedy was a departure from her more serious roles, showcasing a versatile range that echoed her ability to transcend genre boundaries. The Guilt Trip became more than just a film; it was a snapshot of Streisand's willingness to embrace the unexpected and weave it into the fabric of her already storied career.

In the midst of the laughter and the heartfelt moments, Streisand's influence extended beyond the screen. Her role as an executive producer underscored her commitment to shaping narratives, not just for herself but for the broader landscape of storytelling. The collaboration with rising talents like Seth Rogen and established names in the industry showcased her ability to bridge generations, creating a cinematic experience that resonated with audiences young and old.

The success of The Guilt Trip wasn't merely measured in box office numbers; it was a testament to Streisand's enduring relevance in an industry that constantly evolves. As the curtains fell on 2012, the film stood as a reminder that, even after decades in the spotlight, Streisand remained a captivating force, capable of bringing fresh, entertaining narratives to audiences worldwide.

Barbra Streisand's journey in the film industry took an intriguing turn as she geared up for a cinematic adaptation of the beloved musical, Gypsy. This production, boasting music by Jules Styne, a book by Arthur Laurents, and lyrics by the legendary Stephen Sondheim, was set to showcase Streisand's multifaceted talents. The anticipation escalated when Richard LaGravenese was rumored to be on board as the screenwriter.

In a cinematic twist, April of 2016 brought exciting news, revealing that Streisand was not only slated to star in the film but also to take on the role of a producer. The visionary behind the lens, Barry Levinson, was announced as the director, and the film found a home with STX Entertainment for distribution. The stage was set, and by June of the same year, the script had reached its final form, ready to unfold on the big screen in early 2017.

However, the winds of change swept through the project. In a surprising turn of events in 2019, reports surfaced, indicating Streisand's exit from the Gypsy adaptation. The curtain closed on what could have been a spectacular cinematic endeavor, leaving fans and industry insiders intrigued about the untold chapters of this unfulfilled venture.

While the Gypsy project faced unforeseen challenges, Streisand's foray into the director's chair was not limited to that. In 2015, ambitious plans emerged for Streisand to direct a feature biopic centered around the enigmatic 18th-century

Russian empress, Catherine the Great. The project was fueled by the momentum of a top script from the 2014 Black List, masterfully produced by Gil Netter. To add to the allure, the talented Keira Knightley was rumored to take on the regal lead role.

As we dive into these behind-the-scenes glimpses of Streisand's career, one cannot help but marvel at the dynamic range of projects she considered. The Gypsy musical promised a showcase of her performing prowess, while the Catherine the Great biopic hinted at her directorial ambitions. Each project, a potential masterpiece in its own right, held the promise of immersing audiences in the magic of Streisand's creative genius.

Fast forward to the present, and the Catherine the Great biopic remains shrouded in mystery. As of 2022, the plans that once captivated imaginations have yet to materialize on the silver screen. The reasons behind this stall remain undisclosed, leaving fans curious about the fate of a film that seemed destined to merge history, artistry, and Streisand's unique directorial vision.

In the ever-evolving landscape of the entertainment industry, Streisand's ventures exemplify the unpredictable nature of artistic pursuits. From the high notes of successful script completion to the unexpected exits from promising projects, her story mirrors the complexity and uncertainty that define Hollywood.

As we navigate the labyrinth of Streisand's filmography, we find ourselves at a crossroads – a juncture where unfulfilled potential coexists with the brilliance of realized endeavors. The Gypsy musical and the Catherine the Great biopic serve as compelling chapters in a narrative that transcends the screen, embodying the essence of a career marked by ambition, creativity, and the undying pursuit of artistic expression.

The next turn in Streisand's cinematic journey is yet to unfold, and as the reels of time continue to spin, we remain eager spectators, anticipating the next act in the captivating tale of a Hollywood icon.

Chapter 4

Artistry and Impacts

Barbra Streisand, an unparalleled force in the music industry, has captivated audiences with a mezzo-soprano vocal range that can only be described as "peerless," according to Howard Cohen of the Miami Herald. It's a vocal prowess that goes beyond technical skill; it's a journey into the soul of Brooklyn's very own Streisand.

Whitney Balliett, in awe of Streisand's vocal dynamics, noted how she mesmerizes listeners with her shrewd control—from a soft, intimate whisper to an elbowing, loud proclamation. Streisand's vocal acrobatics, including bravura climbs and a rolling vibrato, make her voice an instrument of sheer brilliance. Yet, what truly sets her apart is that unmistakable nasal quality—a Streisand-from-Brooklyn trademark that rivals the immediate recognition of Louis Armstrong's iconic sound.

Intriguingly, Streisand's musical genius goes beyond the mere execution of notes. As music writer Allegra Rossi reveals, Streisand, despite being unable to read or write music, possesses a unique ability to craft complete compositions in her mind. It's as if she hears melodies as fully realized works of art, effortlessly absorbing and interpreting them. Streisand's musical journey is not confined by traditional boundaries; she transcends the limitations of musical notation.

What sets her apart even further is her extraordinary capacity to sustain long notes—an ability she deliberately honed. Streisand's determination to mold a tune in ways others cannot speaks volumes about her dedication to her craft. She navigates the delicate space between song and speech with finesse, maintaining pitch, rhythm, and a profound sense of meaning.

Streisand's vocal artistry is not just about hitting the right notes; it's about storytelling. Her voice becomes a medium through which narratives unfold, and emotions resonate. Whether it's a tender ballad or a powerful anthem, Streisand has an innate ability to connect with her audience on a profound level.

Her Brooklyn roots infuse her vocal delivery with authenticity and grit. Streisand's voice is a testament to her journey—from the streets of Brooklyn to the grand stages of the world. It's a journey that echoes in every note she sings, a celebration of resilience and the unwavering spirit of a woman who dared to dream.

As we delve into the artistry of Barbra Streisand, it becomes evident that her musical brilliance extends beyond technical expertise. It's a holistic experience that encompasses the heart, soul, and streets of Brooklyn. Streisand's voice, like a masterfully crafted instrument, weaves tales of love, loss, and triumph, leaving an indelible mark on the very fabric of musical history.

Barbra Streisand, a powerhouse in the realm of pop music, transcends the ordinary with a voice that goes beyond the expected. Often labeled as "semi-operatic," her vocal prowess is an awe-inspiring fusion of strength and exquisite tone, creating a unique musical experience.

In the symphony of popular tunes, Streisand's voice stands out as a "suspension bridge between old-school belting and microphone pop," as eloquently stated by Adam Feldman of Time Out. This distinctive vocal style is not just a performance; it's a signature that leaves an indelible mark on the ears of her listeners. Picture it as a captivating journey across musical landscapes where tradition meets modernity.

What sets Streisand apart is not just her ability to hit high notes, but the remarkable duality in which she delivers them—whether loud and commanding or soft and intimate. It's a vocal versatility that captivates, drawing in audiences with its dynamic range. Classical pianist Glenn Gould went so far as to declare himself "a Streisand freak," a testament to the magnetic allure of her vocal artistry.

But Streisand's magic extends beyond hitting notes flawlessly; it's in the subtle yet impactful embellishments she weaves into a melodic line. These nuances elevate her performances to a level of sophistication that transcends the boundaries of conventional pop. It's the art of musical storytelling, where each note becomes a brushstroke painting a vivid picture of emotion and expression.

As you embark on the sonic journey of Streisand's artistry, you'll find yourself immersed in a world where each note is not just heard but felt. It's a realm where the boundaries between singer and song blur, leaving room for a profound connection between the artist and the audience.

In the landscape of pop music, Streisand stands as a trailblazer, pushing the boundaries of what a voice can achieve. Her ability to navigate the intricacies of both old-school belting and modern microphone pop is a testament to her enduring influence on the musical panorama. It's a journey that goes beyond the surface, delving into the very soul of her craft.

Critics and audiences alike began noticing a subtle transformation in her voice around 2010, observing that it had "lowered and acquired an occasionally husky edge." Yet, amidst this change, New York Times music critic Stephen Holden astutely recognized that Streisand's distinctive tone and musical instincts persisted. He eloquently stated that she retained "the gift of conveying a primal human longing in a beautiful sound."

In the eyes of Paul Taylor from The Independent, Streisand's vocal texture may have appeared a bit "scratchy and frayed" in recent years. However, he marveled at her stout resolve and superb technique, describing how she managed to hoist her voice over these challenges, making it not only aesthetically impressive but morally so as well. It's a testament to Streisand's resilience and dedication to her craft.

Fast forward to 2014, Streisand graced the music scene with her studio album, "Partners." Gil Naveh of Haaretz, in his review, painted a vivid picture of her voice as "velvety, clear, and powerful." The passing years, he noted, had bestowed upon it a fascinating depth and roughness, adding layers of richness to her already illustrious vocal prowess.

Streisand's ability to navigate the nuances of her changing voice reflects not just an artist, but a storyteller who uses her instrument to convey the complexities of the human experience. It's akin to watching a master painter adapt to new brushes, each stroke adding depth and character to the canvas of her musical legacy.

As we delve deeper into the chapters of Barbra Streisand's biography, it becomes apparent that her journey extends far beyond the spotlight. Her personal life and relationships, explored in the upcoming sections, offer a glimpse into the woman behind the music. It's a tapestry woven with threads of triumphs and challenges, revealing the human side of a global sensation.

Streisand's influence on the entertainment landscape, dissected in the subsequent segment, is nothing short of seismic. Her musical contributions have resonated across generations, creating an indelible mark on the very fabric of pop culture. The stage is set for an exploration of the artistry and impact that define this living legend.

Beyond the melodies, Streisand has been a beacon of philanthropy and activism. Her social contributions, discussed in detail later on, paint a picture of an artist using her platform for meaningful change. It's a narrative that goes beyond the notes and lyrics, showcasing the power of art as a catalyst for a better world.

As we navigate through Streisand's biography, it's essential to acknowledge the legacy she has meticulously crafted. The enduring impact on pop culture, celebrated in the chapters to come, is a testament to her staying power in an ever-evolving industry. Honors and recognitions punctuate this journey, validating not only her talent but also the profound connection she has forged with audiences worldwide.

In the next sections, we will unravel the layers of Barbra Streisand's life, exploring the personal and professional chapters that have shaped her into the living legend we know today. Stay tuned as we delve into the fascinating depth of Barbra Streisand's personal life.

Chapter 5

Personal Life and Relationship

Relationship and Family

Barbra Streisand's journey through relationships has been as fascinating as her illustrious career. Her first venture into marriage was with actor Elliott Gould on September 13, 1963. The glitz of Hollywood couldn't shield their relationship from the complexities of life, leading to an announcement of separation on February 12, 1969, and a final divorce on July 6, 1971. Despite the end of their marital journey, the couple left behind a shared legacy in the form of their son, Jason Gould, who later graced the screen as her on-screen son in the emotionally charged film, The Prince of Tides.

In the late '60s and early '70s, Streisand's love life took an intriguing political turn as she found herself in the company of none other than Canadian Prime Minister Pierre Trudeau. The romance unfolded between 1969 and 1970, adding a political twist to the chapters of her personal life.

However, love took another chance on Barbra when she entered into a relationship with hairdresser and producer Jon Peters in 1973. This wasn't just a romantic connection; it evolved into a professional partnership with Peters taking on roles as her manager and producer. The dynamics of their relationship were put to the test during the making of Yentl, leading to a breakup in 1982. Despite the romantic detour, the two managed to navigate the complexities and emerged as friends. Streisand even embraced the role of godmother to Peters' daughters, Caleigh Peters and Skye Peters, showcasing the enduring bond they share.

The intricacies of Streisand's love life paint a vivid picture of a woman who has experienced the highs and lows of romantic entanglements in the spotlight. From the glitzy world of Hollywood with Elliott Gould to the political intrigue with Pierre Trudeau and the intertwining of love and profession with Jon Peters, each chapter in her relationship journey unfolds like a captivating screenplay.

The spotlight on her love life brightened briefly as she shared a clandestine romance with film director Michael Cimino in the early months of 1983. Their connection, shrouded in secrecy, unfolded against the backdrop of Cimino's consideration of Streisand for a role in his planned adaptation of Ayn Rand's "The Fountainhead," a cinematic endeavor that never materialized.

As the seasons changed, so did the chapters of Streisand's romantic escapades. From November 1983 to October 1987, the melody of her heart played in harmony with composer Richard Baskin. Baskin, the mastermind behind the poignant lyrics of "Here We Are At Last" on her 1984 album "Emotion," shared a home with Streisand during this period, adding a symphonic note to the verses of her personal story.

The winds of love then carried her towards actor Don Johnson, and from December 1987 to at least September 1988, their hearts beat in unison. Their musical collaboration extended beyond mere emotions, culminating in a duet of "Till I Loved You." The echoes of their connection resonated not only in their shared experiences but also in the harmonies of their shared melodies.

In the early '80s, Streisand encountered the brief but intriguing presence of actor Richard Gere in her romantic repertoire. The chemistry that sparked during 1983 left an indelible mark, a fleeting yet memorable encounter in the grand stage of her life. Fast forward to 1989, and Clint Eastwood stepped into her narrative, albeit briefly. Each chapter unfolded like scenes in a cinematic masterpiece, leaving the audience captivated by the star-studded cast of Streisand's love life.

Venturing into the realm of music and passion, the years 1989 to 1991 saw Streisand entwined with the notes and chords of composer James Newton Howard. Their symphony of love played out, creating a chapter of harmony and rhythm in the grand score of her existence. As Streisand moved through these varied romantic encounters, the world witnessed not just the iconic singer but a woman navigating the complex dance of love and connection.

The allure of Streisand's relationships lies not just in the names but in the nuanced melodies each brought to her life. From the clandestine whispers of secrecy with Cimino to the lyrical collaboration with Baskin, the romantic notes with Johnson, Gere, and Eastwood, and the symphonic resonance with Howard, each connection paints a vivid stroke on the canvas of her love story.

In the early '90s, she made headlines with her unexpected romance with tennis icon Andre Agassi. Their unconventional age gap stirred public fascination, yet Agassi unabashedly embraced it, declaring in his 2009 autobiography, *"We agree that we're good for each other, and so what if she's twenty-eight years older? We're simpatico, and the public outcry only adds spice to our connection. It makes our friendship feel forbidden, taboo – another piece of my overall rebellion. Dating Barbra Streisand is like wearing Hot Lava."*

The fiery passion Agassi describes seemed to be a theme in Streisand's romantic life during the early-to-mid-1990s. She ventured into relationships with several high-profile men, leaving the public and media eager to dissect every detail. From the charisma of newscaster Peter Jennings to the magnetic presence of actors Liam Neeson, Jon Voight, and Peter Weller, Streisand's love life became a captivating narrative on its own.

However, the pinnacle of her romantic tale unfolded on July 1, 1998, when Streisand exchanged vows with actor James Brolin, her second husband. Their union was not just a marriage; it was a fusion of two seasoned souls in the spotlight. Despite the lack of biological children between them, Brolin brought a family of his own into their shared journey. With two sons from his first marriage, including the acclaimed actor Josh Brolin, and a daughter from his second marriage, their familial tapestry was as intricate as it was heartwarming.

Away from the glitz and glamour, Streisand found solace in the companionship of her furry friends. Her love for dogs transcended the ordinary, reaching a pinnacle of devotion with her cherished dog, Samantha. So deep was her connection that Streisand made headlines by having Samantha cloned, immortalizing the bond in a way only she could.

Despite the adoration she received, Streisand, like any icon, faced moments of controversy. In March 2019, she found herself issuing a public apology for controversial statements concerning Michael Jackson's accusers. This incident highlighted the complexities of being a public figure and the constant scrutiny that accompanies fame.

As we navigate the intricacies of Barbra Streisand's relationships, we glimpse not just the romance but the vibrant tapestry of a life lived in the limelight. Each chapter unfolds with its unique hues, blending love, companionship, and the inevitable shadows that fame casts. Streisand's story continues to resonate, leaving us eagerly anticipating the next captivating chapter in the life of an icon who has truly worn love and fame like a bespoke garment.

Name

Barbra Streisand's journey into individuality extends beyond the spotlight, delving into the very essence of her identity, starting with a deliberate alteration to her name. At the age of 18, she embarked on a quest for uniqueness, a quest that led to the transformation of "Barbara" into the distinct "Barbra." As she candidly puts it, "I hated the name, but I refused to change it." This declaration carries with it the rebellious spirit that would come to define her approach to both life and art.

In recounting this pivotal decision, Streisand unveils the intricate thought process that fueled her choice. "I wanted to be unique, but I didn't want to change my name because that was too false," she reflects. The pressure to conform was real, with suggestions like "Joanie Sands" floating around. Yet, true to her nature, she resisted the conventional and found a compromise that spoke to her authenticity. "No, let's see, if I take out the 'a,' it's still 'Barbara,' but it's unique." The modification became a symbol of her refusal to succumb to societal expectations, a subtle rebellion etched into the letters of her name.

A 1967 biography, accompanied by a concert program, sheds further light on this act of linguistic defiance, noting that the alteration in the spelling of her first name was a deliberate act of rebellion. Advised to change her last name, she countered by shedding an "a" from the first, a subtle but significant declaration of independence.

Beyond her first name, Streisand's surname carries its own narrative. Pronounced with an "s" sound, "like sand on the beach," she asserts, it distinguishes itself from the more commonly heard "z" sound. This nuance in pronunciation is not merely a linguistic quirk but a reflection of her meticulous attention to detail, a refusal to let even the phonetic elements of her name conform to the expected.

Even in the digital realm, Streisand remains vigilant about the correct pronunciation of her surname. When the Apple voice digital assistant Siri erred in pronouncing her name, she took matters into her own hands. Contacting none other than Apple CEO Tim Cook, she voiced her concern, and Cook promptly ensured the correction. This incident serves as a testament to her unwavering commitment to accuracy and her willingness to stand up for what she believes, even in the face of technological missteps.

Politics

In the early stages of her remarkable career, Barbra Streisand's political leanings weren't at the forefront of her pursuits. However, a pivotal shift occurred in 1968 when her activism took center stage. Notably, she passionately supported the presidential campaign of Eugene McCarthy, a prominent figure advocating an anti–Vietnam War stance.

During July of that transformative year, Streisand, alongside luminaries like Harry Belafonte, graced the Hollywood Bowl in a fundraising concert sponsored by the Southern Christian Leadership Conference. The aim was clear: to benefit the impoverished sections of society, demonstrating Streisand's early commitment to social causes.

As her political engagement intensified, Streisand emerged as a stalwart supporter of the Democratic Party and its various causes. Notably, her involvement earned her a spot on President Richard Nixon's 1971 list of political enemies, a testament to the strength of her convictions.

In 1972, amidst a political landscape dominated by anti-war sentiments, Streisand threw her considerable influence behind George McGovern's presidential campaign. Headlining the benefit concert "Four for McGovern," organized by the dynamic duo of actor Warren Beatty and record producer Lou Adler, Streisand's electrifying performance was immortalized in the release of "Live Concert at the Forum." The event marked a pivotal moment in her political activism, showcasing her commitment to causes that resonated with her values.

The following year, Streisand collaborated with liberal activist Stanley Sheinbaum and the American Civil Liberties Union for a noteworthy cause. Hosting a benefit at the opulent mansion of film mogul Jennings Lang, the aim was to raise funds for the legal defense of Daniel Ellsberg, the whistleblower of Pentagon Papers fame. Accompanied by a talented combo featuring Marvin Hamlisch on piano, Streisand not only entertained a star-studded audience but also took paid song requests from attendees and via telephone, culminating in an impressive $50,000 in funds for Ellsberg's defense.

Streisand's foray into politics wasn't merely a series of performances; it was a deliberate and impactful choice to align herself with causes that resonated with her values. Her ability to seamlessly integrate her artistic prowess with political activism not only spoke volumes about her commitment but also endeared her to those who shared similar convictions.

As the turbulent political landscape continued to shape the narrative of the time, Streisand's involvement became synonymous with standing up for principles that transcended entertainment. The intertwining of her artistry with activism painted a vivid picture of an artist who recognized the power of her platform and used it to effect change.

In 1984, she, along with Jane Fonda and other industry luminaries, founded the Hollywood Women's Political Committee (HWPC), a dynamic activist group that swelled to 300 members. Their impact resonated beyond Hollywood, playing a pivotal role in the Democratic Party's ascension to majority control in the 1986 U.S. Senate elections.

As the HWPC thrived, Streisand's influence extended to the political landscape. In 1992, she lent her support to Bill Clinton's presidential election, a move that contributed to the seismic shift in American politics known as the Year of the Woman. The election ushered in a wave of women senators, reflecting Streisand's commitment to empowering women in politics.

Harvard's John F. Kennedy School of Government became a platform for Streisand in 1995. Here, she eloquently addressed the role of the artist as a citizen, passionately advocating for arts programs and funding. Streisand's voice resonated not only as a renowned entertainer but as a champion for the arts and their vital role in society.

Streisand's advocacy expanded to embrace the LGBTQ+ community. Her active support for LGBT rights manifested in her backing of the "No on 8" campaign, a valiant effort against the regressive California Proposition 8 of 2008. Even in defeat, Streisand's unwavering commitment to equality shone through.

In 2012, Streisand turned her attention to voting rights, decrying laws mandating photo IDs at the polls. She asserted that such laws were designed to disenfranchise elderly and minority citizens, a stance rooted in her belief that voting is a precious right that should be safeguarded. Streisand's passionate denouncement framed these laws not merely as bureaucratic measures but as threats to the very fabric of American democracy.

Fast forward to 2020, and Streisand's dedication to voter rights remained undiminished. A tweet from her directed followers to VoteRiders, a nonprofit organization assisting citizens in obtaining the necessary identification to exercise their right to vote. Streisand's continued involvement underscores her enduring commitment to the democratic process.

In June 2013, she marked her presence at the 90th birthday celebration of Shimon Peres in Jerusalem. The international convention center served as a backdrop to Streisand's participation, where she not only attended but lent her melodic voice to two concerts in Tel Aviv that same week as part of her inaugural concert tour in Israel. It wasn't just a performance; it was a testament to her global engagement and celebration of milestones transcending borders.

Fast forward to January 2017, Streisand found herself amidst the sea of voices at the 2017 Women's March in Los Angeles. Introduced by Rufus Wainwright, her presence on stage was more than symbolic; it was a statement. In a stirring speech, Streisand echoed the collective sentiments of the march, a powerful display of solidarity and a call for change. It was a moment that highlighted her commitment to causes that resonate with the heartbeat of societal movements.

The political undertones in Streisand's life took a more explicit turn in an October 2018 interview with Emma Brockes of The Guardian. Here, she delved into the thematic core of her album "Walls." In a candid expression of her concerns, Streisand unveiled her apprehensions about then-President Donald Trump and the perceived threats he posed to the very fabric of the United States. Her words resonated with a sense of urgency, describing the times as "dangerous" and emphasizing the need for collective action.

"This is a dangerous time in this nation, this republic: a man who is corrupt and indecent and is assaulting our institutions. It's really, really frightening. And I just pray that people who are compassionate and respect the truth will come out and vote. I'm saying more than just vote. Vote for Democrats!" Streisand's statement was a departure from the neutrality often expected from entertainers. Instead, it was a clarion call, a plea for conscientious participation in the democratic process.

In dissecting Streisand's political engagement, it becomes evident that her commitment goes beyond the superficial. It's not merely about attending events or making statements—it's a genuine concern for the well-being of the nation she holds dear. Her involvement in the Women's March showcased her solidarity with issues affecting women, while her outspokenness against perceived threats to democracy in the Trump era demonstrated a deep-seated commitment to truth and justice.

Streisand's journey through the political landscape is marked by a willingness to leverage her influence for the greater good. It's a testament to the idea that artistry doesn't exist in a vacuum; it's intertwined with the social and political currents of the time. The iconic performer isn't just a spectator; she's an active participant in shaping the narrative.

As we navigate through the chapters of Streisand's life, it becomes clear that her political engagement isn't a fleeting dalliance—it's an integral part of her story. The stage isn't just a platform for her musical prowess; it's a podium for advocacy and a call to action. In a world where entertainers often tiptoe around political issues, Streisand stands out as a bold voice unafraid to use her influence for the greater good.

The echoes of her words continue to reverberate—a call for compassion, respect for truth, and an impassioned plea for active participation in the democratic process. Streisand's political journey is a compelling narrative that adds depth to her legacy, showcasing that the pursuit of art and the pursuit of a better world can harmoniously coexist.

Chapter 6

Philanthropy and Activism

Barbra Streisand's philanthropic endeavors stand as a testament to her commitment to making a positive impact on the world. In 1984, she bestowed the Emanuel Streisand Building for Jewish Studies upon the Hebrew University of Jerusalem, a poignant tribute to her father, an esteemed educator and scholar. This act of generosity not only commemorates her father's legacy but also exemplifies Streisand's deep-rooted connection to her heritage.

The songstress's philanthropic influence extends far beyond the borders of Jerusalem. Through her live performances, Streisand has personally spearheaded fundraising efforts, amassing an impressive $25 million for various charitable organizations. The magnitude of her impact is not just measured in dollars but in the tangible change these funds bring to causes close to her heart.

At the heart of Streisand's philanthropic initiatives is the Streisand Foundation, a beacon of hope established in 1986. With a dedicated focus on preserving the environment, voter education, civil liberties, civil rights, women's issues, and nuclear disarmament, the foundation has been a driving force for positive change. Through nearly 1,000 grants, totaling over $16 million, it has empowered national organizations to champion these critical causes. Streisand's foundation acts as a catalyst for progress, igniting change where it is needed most.

In the ever-evolving landscape of global challenges, Streisand has consistently demonstrated her commitment to addressing pressing issues. Her $1 million donation to the William J. Clinton Foundation in 2006 showcased her support for former President Bill Clinton's climate change initiative. This substantial contribution reflects Streisand's understanding of the importance of collective action in tackling environmental issues on a global scale.

What sets Streisand's philanthropy apart is not just the financial support she provides but the genuine passion and advocacy she brings to each cause. Her involvement goes beyond cutting a check; it's about using her platform to amplify the voices of those fighting for a better world. Streisand has become a champion for the environment, a vocal advocate for civil liberties, and a supporter of women's rights.

As an artist who has touched the hearts of millions through her music and performances, Streisand leverages her fame to shed light on issues that demand our attention. Her commitment to nuclear disarmament is not just a line on a grant application; it's a reflection of her belief in a safer and more peaceful world. Streisand's philanthropy is woven into the fabric of her identity, an integral part of who she is as an individual and an artist.

In 2009, she demonstrated her dedication to women's health by generously endowing the Barbra

Streisand Women's Cardiovascular Research and Education Program at Cedars-Sinai Medical Center's Women's Heart Center with a substantial $5 million donation. This initiative aimed at advancing cardiovascular research and education, showcasing Streisand's passion for contributing to the betterment of healthcare.

Streisand's philanthropic spirit didn't go unnoticed. Parade magazine, in its Giving Back 30 survey, recognized her as the third most generous celebrity in 2007. The Giving Back Fund highlighted her remarkable contributions, noting a significant $11 million donation, all of which was distributed by The Streisand Foundation. It's not just about the numbers; Streisand's commitment to giving back resonates with the genuine desire to make a positive impact on society.

In 2012, Streisand's dedication to women's cardiovascular health reached new heights. She orchestrated a remarkable fundraising effort, raising an impressive $22 million to further support the Barbra Streisand Women's Heart Center. Her personal contribution of $10 million underscored her unwavering commitment to the cause. This center, bearing her name, stands as a testament to Streisand's enduring legacy in promoting women's health.

Beyond the world of healthcare, Streisand's charitable contributions extend to her personal interests. A renowned collector of art and furniture, she decided to part with 526 items at Julien's Auctions in October 2009. The entire proceeds from this auction were directed to her foundation, showcasing her willingness to leverage her passions for the greater good. Notable items included a costume from "Funny Lady" and a vintage dental cabinet, a nostalgic piece from Streisand's own past. In December 2011, Streisand took her philanthropy to international heights by participating in a fundraising gala for Israel Defense Forces charities. This global outlook emphasizes her commitment to supporting causes that transcend borders and impact lives on a global scale.

The year 2020 marked another instance of Streisand's compassion and generosity. In the wake of George Floyd's tragic death, she extended her support to his daughter, Gianna Floyd, by gifting her Disney shares. This gesture highlighted Streisand's empathy and desire to stand in solidarity with those affected by social injustices.

Fast forward to September 22, 2022, when Barbra Streisand received a unique invitation from Volodymyr Zelenskyy, the president of Ukraine. Recognizing her as a force for positive change, Zelenskyy invited Streisand to become an ambassador for the UNITED24 platform, specifically focusing on the Medical Aid direction of support. Streisand's involvement helped raise a substantial $240,000 for medical care, once again showcasing her ability to mobilize support for critical causes.

Barbra Streisand's philanthropic journey is not just about financial contributions; it's about using her influence to create meaningful change. As she continues to champion various causes, her legacy extends beyond the stage and screen, leaving an indelible mark on the world.

Chapter 7

Legacy

Barbra Streisand, the indomitable force in the world of music and entertainment, has left an indelible mark on the industry, earning her the well-deserved title of the "Queen of the Divas." In a realm where talent is revered, Streisand's influence transcends generations, making her a living legend in the pantheon of American music.

The New York Times, ever the arbiter of cultural significance, places Streisand among America's Most Beloved Divas, sharing the throne with none other than Dolly Parton and Patti Labelle. This triumvirate of extraordinary talent speaks volumes about Streisand's enduring appeal and universal acclaim.

Vulture, in paying homage to her timeless contributions, aptly notes that Streisand's influence extends far beyond her immediate contemporaries. Her artistic footprint can be traced in the works of icons like Céline Dion, the 1980s output of Lionel Richie and Luther Vandross, and the emotionally charged ballads of Mariah Carey, Adele, and Whitney Houston. Streisand's impact is not just a chapter in the history of music; it's a narrative that continues to shape the very essence of the industry.

Forbes recognizes Streisand as the "Queen of the Charts," a testament to her unparalleled longevity on the Billboard charts. Her songs, like enduring classics, have weathered the storms of changing trends, proving that true artistry is timeless. Streisand's chart-topping success is not merely a fleeting moment; it's a saga of musical prowess etched in the annals of American music history.

The Los Angeles Times, a stalwart in chronicling cultural revolutions, bestows upon Streisand the titles of the "most influential female vocalist" and the "most revolutionary of performers." She isn't just a singer; she's a trailblazer who redefined the rules for female performers, setting a standard that others aspire to reach. Streisand's impact is not confined to her vocal range; it's a cultural shift that has paved the way for generations of female artists.

CNN, recognizing the romantic allure in her voice, places Streisand among the most romantic singers of the 20th century. Her ability to evoke emotion through her music is a testament to the depth of her artistry, creating a connection with audiences that transcends time. Streisand's voice is not just a melody; it's a symphony of emotions that resonates with the hearts of listeners.

In 2023, Rolling Stone, the vanguard of music journalism, affirms her enduring legacy by ranking Streisand at number 147 on its list of the 200 Greatest Singers of All Time. This accolade is not just a recognition of her past achievements; it's an acknowledgment of her ongoing influence that reverberates through the corridors of musical greatness.

Taking a stroll down memory lane to 1997, New York magazine applauds Streisand's fashion sense, noting that she embarked on a surreal, chameleonic, personal fashion quest. Her sartorial choices weren't just about clothes; they were a revolutionary statement that ignited the retro revolution in the 1960s. Streisand wasn't just a trendsetter; she was a fashion maven whose style transcended time and left an indelible mark on the industry.

Honour

Barbra Streisand's legacy isn't just about her incredible talent on the stage and screen; it's a tapestry woven with honors, awards, and recognitions that reflect the profound impact she has had on various realms. As we journey through the pages of her illustrious career, the accolades she has received form a testament to her enduring commitment to excellence and her influential presence in the entertainment industry.

In 1964, Mademoiselle bestowed upon her the Distinguished Merit Award, setting the stage for a trailblazing career. The following year, Streisand was not merely recognized but celebrated as Miss Ziegfeld in 1965. The crescendo of accolades continued in 1968 when she was awarded the Israel Freedom Medal, the highest civilian honor in Israel. This was a poignant acknowledgment of her contributions, transcending geographical boundaries.

The rhythm of recognition kept playing in tune with her achievements. In 1969, ASCAP honored her with the Pied Piper Award, and she received the

Prix De L'Academie Charles Cros, adding an international flair to her growing collection of accolades. The City of New York itself, her hometown, presented her with the Crystal Apple, a symbol of their pride in her accomplishments. Streisand's impact was not limited to entertainment; the Anti-Defamation League acknowledged her as a Woman of Achievement in the Arts in 1978, underlining her multifaceted influence.

The melody of honors reached a new pitch in 1984 when Streisand received the Women in Film Crystal Award. This accolade was not just about her achievements but recognized her endurance, emphasizing the pivotal role women play within the entertainment industry. As the applause echoed, Streisand's legacy continued to crescendo.

The rhythm of her impact extended beyond borders and across various realms of society. The National Organization for Women (NOW) recognized her with the Woman of Courage Award, solidifying her stance as a symbol of empowerment. The Ordre des Arts et des Lettres and Scopus Award from American Friends of the Hebrew University added an international and academic touch to her accolades, showcasing the breadth of her influence.

In 1991, Streisand was acknowledged for breaking ground in filmmaking at the Women, Men and Media symposium, receiving Breakthrough Awards for "making films that portray women with serious complexity." Her commitment to societal causes echoed loud and clear in 1992 when she received the Commitment to Life Award from AIDS Project Los Angeles (APLA) and the Bill of Rights Award from the American Civil Liberties Union of Southern California.

Her impact on the cinematic landscape was not just acknowledged but celebrated with the Dorothy Arzner Special Recognition by Women in Film and the Golden Plate by the Academy of Achievement in 1992. The year 1994 brought the resonant Harry Chapin Humanitarian Award from the ASCAP and the Peabody Award, a testament to her commitment to humanitarian causes. The same year, Brandeis University honored her with an Honorary Doctorate in Arts and Humanities, further solidifying her influence across disciplines.

As the curtain fell on 1995, Streisand's accomplishments continued to shine with the Filmmaker of the Year Award for "lifetime achievement in filmmaking" by ShowEast and another Peabody Award in 1996. The rhythm persisted, with the Christopher Award in 1998, marking a continued celebration of her profound impact on the world of entertainment and beyond.

Picture this: the year 2000, a momentous occasion where President Bill Clinton, standing on the grand stage of national acclaim, bestows upon Streisand the National Medal of Arts. This, my friends, is the pinnacle of recognition for artistic achievement, a testament to her prowess in an industry that thrives on brilliance. It's not just a medal; it's a symbol of her enduring impact on the cultural tapestry of America.

But that's not where the accolades end. Enter the Library of Congress Living Legend distinction, a title that immortalizes Streisand as a living embodiment of legendary status. The American Film Institute, recognizing her monumental career in film, raises a toast to her with the prestigious AFI Life Achievement Award. Imagine the weight of those words – life achievement – encapsulating a career that has shaped the very essence of cinema.

Let's fast forward to 2007 when French President Nicolas Sarkozy, with an air of admiration, presents Streisand with the Legion of Honour, the highest decoration in France. Now, that's not just an award; it's a recognition transcending borders, a nod to her global impact on the world of arts and culture.

Hold your breath, for President George W. Bush steps into the spotlight, honoring Streisand with the Kennedy Center Honors in 2007. It's not just an acknowledgment; it's a celebration of cultural triumphs that echo through the hallowed halls of artistic achievement.

And then, the journey continues into the 21st century. In 2011, the Board of Governors Humanitarian Award finds its way into Streisand's hands, recognizing not only her efforts for women's heart health but also her extensive philanthropic endeavors. The L'Oréal Paris Legend Award in the 18th Elle Magazine Women in Hollywood further cements her status as a legend in the realms of both beauty and talent.

As the pages turn, 2012 brings forth a Lifetime Achievement Award from the Women Film Critics

Circle, acknowledging her profound impact on the cinematic landscape. The Hebrew University of Jerusalem confers upon her an Honorary Doctorate of Philosophy in 2013, a testament to her intellectual contributions beyond the stage and screen.

But let's delve deeper into 2013 – the year Streisand stood tall as the sole female artist to direct, write, produce, and star in the same major studio film, Yentl. The Film Society of Lincoln Center, recognizing this unparalleled achievement, presents her with the Charlie Chaplin Award for Lifetime Achievement. Oh, and let's not forget the Lifetime Achievement Glamour Awards, a dazzling testament to her enduring glamour and influence.

In 2014, she graced one of the eight New York Magazine covers commemorating a century of pop music in the city. It was a visual celebration of her impact on the cultural landscape, an artist whose influence reverberated through the decades.

Notably, the American Society of Cinematographers (ASC) bestowed upon Streisand the prestigious Board of Governors Award, recognizing her cinematic prowess. Her leadership qualities were further acknowledged when she received the Sherry Lansing Leadership Award at The Hollywood Reporter's annual Women in Entertainment Breakfast. Undoubtedly, Streisand's multifaceted talent was not confined to a single medium; she effortlessly conquered both film and music.

In a moment that solidified her iconic status, Streisand clinched the top spot in the 1010 Wins

Iconic Celebrity Poll by CBS in 2015. Her resonance with the audience was not just a fleeting trend but a lasting connection that spanned generations. President Barack Obama, recognizing her monumental impact, announced in November 2015 that Streisand would receive the Presidential Medal of Freedom, the highest civilian honor in the United States. It was a moment of national recognition for an artist whose influence transcended boundaries.

Streisand's imprint on the entertainment industry is enshrined in various prestigious halls of fame. From her induction into the Hollywood Walk of Fame in 1976 to her recognition in the Goldmine Hall of Fame in 2002, she left an indelible mark. The Long Island Music Hall of Fame welcomed her in 2007, followed by the Hit Parade Hall of Fame in 2009. The National Museum of American Jewish History and California Hall of Fame proudly embraced her in 2010. Each accolade signifies not just success but a lasting impact on the cultural fabric.

In the realm of theater, Streisand's achievements were equally stellar. In 1970, she was honored with a Special Tony Award, rightfully earning the title "Star of the Decade." The National Association of Theatre Owners (NATO) echoed this sentiment in 1980, selecting her once again as the "Star of the Decade." These accolades were not mere reflections of fleeting popularity but acknowledgments of an enduring legacy.

Streisand's influence reached beyond the realms of entertainment, capturing the hearts of the public across diverse demographics. In 1988, she was bestowed with the "President's Award" by NARM, a testament to her cultural impact. The People's Choice Awards recognized her as the "All-Time Favorite Musical Performer" that same year, underscoring her cross-generational appeal.

As the 20th century drew to a close, Streisand's legacy continued to flourish. In 1998, the Harris Poll affirmed her status as the "Most Popular Singer Among Adult Americans of All Ages." The recognition extended to VH1's 100 Greatest Women of Rock N Roll and Mojo magazine's Top 100 Singers of All Time. In a Reuters/Zogby poll, she was named the century's best female singer, a sentiment echoed by the Recording Industry Association of America, which crowned her the "Top Female Artist of the Century" in 1999.

The year 2006 witnessed Streisand standing among the honorees at Oprah Winfrey's white-tie Legends Ball, a gathering of luminaries celebrating cultural contributions. These honors not only recognize her achievements but also serve as a testament to the enduring impact of an artist whose influence spans decades.

In 2015, The Daily Telegraph positioned her among the elite, ranking her among the top 10 female singer-songwriters of all time. A&E's Biography magazine echoed this sentiment, hailing her as one of their favorite leading actresses in the annals of entertainment.

What sets Streisand apart isn't just her vocal prowess; it's the cinematic magic she weaves. She graced the Voices of the Century list by BBC and secured her place on People's "100 Greatest Movie Stars of Time" compilation. VH1 acknowledged her as one of the "200 Greatest Pop Culture Icons of All Time," and Entertainment Weekly bestowed upon her the title of the "Greatest Movie Star of all time," ranking her at an impressive #13.

Billboard recognized Streisand not only for her musical prowess but also for her cultural significance. She holds the prestigious title of the top female Jewish musician of all time, an accolade that solidifies her impact on the industry. The LGBTQ+ community embraced her as a gay icon, with The Advocate listing her among the "25 Coolest Women" and Out magazine dubbing her one of the "12 Greatest Female Gay Icons of All Time."

As the 21st century unfolded, the American Film Institute celebrated a century of cinematic greatness, and Streisand's contributions echoed through time. AFI's 100 Years ... 100 Songs immortalized four of her masterpieces, with "The Way We Were," "Evergreen (Love Theme From A Star Is Born)," "People," and "Don't Rain on My Parade" securing spots in the pantheon of "America's Greatest Music in the Movies."

Streisand's cinematic legacy continued its march through AFI's 100 Years ... series. What's Up, Doc? elicited laughter, earning the 61st spot in AFI's 100 Years ... 100 Laughs. The romance of her films resonated in AFI's 100 Years ... 100 Passions, where The Way We Were, Funny Girl, and What's Up,

Doc? claimed spots at #8, #41, and #68, respectively. Her contribution to the world of movie musicals was duly recognized, with Funny Girl securing the 16th spot in AFI's Greatest Movie Musicals.

The Library of Congress, recognizing the cultural significance of Streisand's work, selected Funny Girl for preservation in the National Film Registry in December 2016. This honor was followed by the inclusion of "People" in the National Recording Registry in March 2017, an acknowledgment that left Streisand humbled as her song became part of the nation's cultural tapestry.

Barbra Streisand's legacy isn't just a collection of accolades; it's a rich tapestry woven with musical notes, cinematic brilliance, and cultural resonance. As we delve deeper into the chapters of her remarkable journey, it becomes evident that her impact transcends time, leaving an indelible mark on the very fabric of entertainment history.

Professional Membership

Barbra Streisand's professional journey is nothing short of extraordinary, spanning across multiple facets of the entertainment industry. She stands as a powerhouse, a multifaceted talent whose influence extends beyond the stage and screen. As we delve into her legacy, one cannot overlook her extensive professional memberships, which further solidify her unparalleled status.

In a league of her own, Streisand holds a unique distinction as the only artist concurrently affiliated with prestigious organizations. Her membership in the American Society of Composers, Authors and Publishers (ASCAP) showcases her musical prowess, underlining her significant contributions to the world of composition. Simultaneously, she's an integral part of the Screen Actors Guild (SAG), where her impact on the cinematic landscape is recognized and celebrated.

Not confined to a single medium, Streisand effortlessly extends her reach to the American Federation of Television and Radio Artists (AFTRA). Her versatile talent seamlessly bridges the gap between different forms of media, making her an influential figure across various platforms. This diversity in her professional affiliations reflects the breadth of her skills, from acting and singing to directing and producing.

As a trailblazer in the film industry, Streisand is a distinguished member of the Academy of Motion Pictures Arts and Sciences. Her cinematic achievements have left an indelible mark, earning her a place among the elite in the world of filmmaking. Additionally, she proudly holds membership in the Actors' Equity Association, highlighting her commitment to the craft of acting on stage.

Beyond the realm of entertainment, Barbra Streisand takes on a meaningful role as the honorary chairwoman of the board of directors of Hadassah's International Research Institute on Women. This philanthropic involvement showcases her dedication to causes beyond the spotlight, emphasizing the importance of research and advocacy for women's issues.

In unraveling the layers of Streisand's professional memberships, we witness a woman who has not merely excelled in one discipline but has conquered the diverse realms of creativity, activism, and leadership. Her legacy, deeply rooted in these affiliations, speaks volumes about the impact she has made and continues to make across the spectrum of the arts.

Conclusion

As we reach the final crescendo of Barbra Streisand's extraordinary biography, it's impossible not to reflect on the incredible journey we've undertaken together. Your investment of time and curiosity has added depth and meaning to the pages that chronicle the life of an American icon—an artist, an advocate, and an indomitable force in the world of entertainment.

In delving into the intricacies of Streisand's narrative, we've traversed the highs and lows of a life lived with passion and purpose. From the smoky nightclubs of New York City to the glitzy glamour of Broadway and the silver screen, every chapter resonates with the echoes of resilience, determination, and an unwavering commitment to excellence. Streisand's story isn't just about fame and fortune; it's a testament to the power of dreams, the pursuit of artistry, and the impact one person can have on the world.

But here's the truth: without your engagement, this biography is just words on paper. It's your curiosity, your willingness to explore the tapestry of Streisand's life, that has given these pages life. Each sentence, each anecdote, gains significance because of the connection forged between the storyteller and the reader. It's your presence that transforms a mere biography into a shared experience, a journey we undertake together.

So, from the bottom of my heart, I want to express my deepest appreciation. Thank you for being a part of this exploration, for allowing the magic of Streisand's life to unfold in your imagination. Your commitment to delving into the intricacies of this remarkable story is what makes the journey worthwhile. You are the heartbeat of this narrative—the rhythm that propels the tale forward. As we bid adieu to the enthralling chapters of Barbra Streisand's life, I'd like to extend a humble request. Your support means the world to us. If this biography has left a mark on you, if the story of Streisand has resonated in your heart, please consider leaving a positive review. Share your thoughts, your insights, and your reflections. Your words have the power to inspire others to embark on this same captivating journey.

In the grand finale of Streisand's biography, let's celebrate not just the end of a story but the beginning of a shared experience. Together, we've danced through the highs and lows, the laughter and tears, and emerged richer for the journey. As we part ways, I hope the echoes of Streisand's life continue to reverberate in your thoughts, a melody that lingers long after the final page is turned. Thank you for being a part of this unforgettable exploration—a journey that wouldn't be the same without you.

Made in United States
North Haven, CT
16 December 2023

45976491R00065